IMAGINARY IDEAS OF CHRIST:

A Scottish-American Debate

JOHN K. LaSHELL

To Bill

Enjoy —

John K. La Shell

ISBN-13: 978-1548503703

IMAGINARY IDEAS OF CHRIST:

A SCOTTISH-AMERICAN DEBATE

by

John K. La Shell

A Dissertation Submitted to the Faculty of

WESTMINSTER THEOLOGICAL SEMINARY

in Partial Fulfillment of the
Requirements for the Degree

DOCTOR OF PHILOSOPHY

1985

Faculty Advisor: _____

Second Faculty Reader: _____

Chairman of the Field Committee: _____

TABLE OF CONTENTS

ACKNOWLEDGEMENTS

I used to think that expressions of gratitude to an author's family were formal pleasantries—expected, but not really necessary. I now have ample evidence that is not true. The last few years have been difficult for them at times. The move across country to attend Westminster was not easy, and long hours with my books or computer have taken their toll on family togetherness. I am thankful that these things have usually been accepted with grace and good humor, a great deal of humor at times. What will we use as the butt of family jokes once the dissertation is accepted? More specifically, I appreciate the careful and persistent proofreading of the manuscript by my wife, Heather.

Two professors at Westminster have made direct contributions to the development of my topic. Dr. Samuel T. Logan gave me my first systematic introduction to Jonathan Edwards in a class which explored Edwards' theology through a study of his major works. Post-Reformation Developments under Dr. D. Clair Davis afforded an opportunity to write the paper which has been expanded into the present dissertation. To both of these men I say, "Thank you, not only for your classes, but also for your counsel."

I also desire to express my appreciation to the staff of the library at Westminster, and particularly to Grace Mullen. Most of my dissertation research has been done in a small town far from an adequate library. Without their patient help, both on campus and through the mailing of many volumes, my work simply could not have been done. Such specific contributions, and the loving encouragement of family and friends lend fresh significance to the ancient words, "What do you have that you did not receive? And if you did receive it, why do you boast as if you had not received it?" (1 Corinthians 4:7). God gives to His people through others as well as directly, and therefore, I gladly return thanks above all to Him.

JESUS IS BEYOND IMAGINATION
Don Wyrtzen

Jesus is beyond imagination,
His beauty is beyond my fantasy;
My mind cannot begin to see how great He is,
My vision cannot grasp eternity.
Jesus is beyond imagination,
His excellence inspires my heart to sing;
My heart is filled with wonder when I think of Him,
For Jesus is my Lord, the King of kings.

Jesus is beyond imagination,
There's no one in this world who can compare;
Mere things on earth begin to lose all meaning,
Before this Prince of Glory, bright and fair.
Jesus is beyond imagination,
This great Shepherd is the Friend of friends to me;
He is the King, the bright and Morning Star—
Preeminent, He reigns sov'reignly.

Jesus is beyond imagination,
My tho'ts will be of Him for countless days;
Hallelujahs will echo through eternity
As countless angels sing my Jesus praise!

3

INTRODUCTION

Great Britain is separated from the United States of America by several thousand miles of salt water. That distance has not changed much over the past three hundred years, but in some senses colonial America was much nearer to the British Isles than the United States is today. It was nearer then in spite of the fact that our world has shrunk dramatically in recent decades. Satellite communications have reduced distances from months to microseconds, but the gap between peoples has often increased.

We now see ourselves as two distinct nations, but when Jonathan Edwards and George Whitefield were lads, they shared the same king. News from across the seas might have been a bit exotic, but it did not constitute "foreign affairs." Although America was in the process of changing, the colonies and the mother country were long held together by a common culture. Nowhere was that more evident than in the cultivation of the human spirit. It was the age of letter writing, and men who had never seen each other could be bound by strong ties of mutual affection and esteem. Opinions voiced on one side of the Atlantic were often of immediate concern on the opposite shore, and if there was no television, perhaps the printed page was nearly as potent.

Factors such as these make it possible to view the Evangelical Awakening in New England and Scotland as one movement rather than two. During the seventeen forties, the opinions of Jonathan Edwards were both respected and vilified by readers north of Hadrian's wall. When visions broke out during the Scottish revival, it was only natural that Edwards' evaluation of them would seem immediately relevant. If Edwards defended such experiences as ideas inevitably impressed on the imaginations of certain people, then both opponents and advocates of the revival had to take notice. And notice they did.

It is the purpose of this study to trace the development of the controversy over "imaginary ideas" of Christ. The impetus for the dispute came from the pen of Jonathan Edwards, but the battle was actually fought in the Scottish press. The first two chapters deal with the rise and spread of what many were pleased to call "enthusiasm." Visions which were reported by a few subjects of the revival required interpretation. The explanation offered by Edwards is examined in chapter three. His theory of imaginary ideas found its most vocal Scottish defender in James Robe. Robe's writings proved to be a lightning rod, attracting the fire of evangelical ministers in the Scottish Secession Church. Opposition to Edwards' understanding of visions came first from Adam Gib, but the major work on the subject was written by Ralph Erskine. In chapter four the interchange between Robe and Erskine is examined in detail. The final chapter of the dissertation provides an evaluation of the controversy and suggests how the theory of "imaginary ideas" may be relevant to the preaching of Edwards and Erskine, as well as to the present day.

Perhaps one word of caution should be added. Since the study concentrates on the aberrations which surfaced during the Evangelical Awakening, it may be easy to forget the refreshing currents of spiritual water which flowed from newly opened springs in those days. It is the present writer's conviction that the revival was, in the main, a mighty work of the Holy Spirit. Therefore, some justification may be required for focusing attention on the irregularities of the movement. Two reasons may be given. First, although Edwards and Erskine come to opposite conclusions, nevertheless, both make significant contributions to the interpretation of the phenomena. Second, similar problems have frequently accompanied periods of spiritual renewal down to the present day. Insights gained by men of God in the past can ill afford to be lost, and it is hoped that renewed study will aid in their recovery.

CHAPTER 1
VISIONS IN NEW ENGLAND

Foretaste of Things to Come

And it shall come to pass afterward, that I will pour out my spirit upon all flesh; and your sons and your daughters shall prophesy, your old men shall dream dreams, your young men shall see visions: And also upon the servants and upon the handmaids in those days will I pour out my spirit (Joel 2:28-29).

In the heady days of the early seventeen forties it seemed to many in New England that the words of the prophet were receiving a grand fulfillment. The "city set on a hill" over a century before was beginning to shed its light on the rest of the world. Surely the millennium could not be far behind. What did it matter if a largely unconverted ministry blasphemed the marvelous work of the Spirit? God would soon vindicate His true servants. What He had declared to them in secret would be blazoned before the whole world. In flaming judgment, He would come to wreak horrible destruction on the unrepentant and to set up the eternal kingdom of the saints.

The first three decades of the century gave little hint of the conflagration that was to come. Religion in New England had for some time been in a state of decline. The spiritual fervor of the early colonists had degenerated into pious moralism encased in a shell of traditional religious phraseology.

[Calvinistic Christianity] was not being effectively disputed, nor was it being openly discarded. It was simply being ignored as a matter of little consequence for practical living, by men who said one thing and did another. New England was becoming involved in the ways of the Old World, striving for commercial success, competing for profits, tasting power and assuming rights, ready to defend them legally or otherwise.... The theocentric piety of Calvinism seemed doomed (Haroutunian 1932, xx-xxi).

Colonial ministers were not unaware of the decline. The standard form of declamation against national sin was the jeremiad, a stylized reminder of the covenanted privileges and responsibilities of New England along with suitable threats of providential judgment for failure to repent. Developed during the last half of the seventeenth century, the jeremiad experienced a powerful resurgence during the centennial discourses of 1730 (Miller 1953, 482-484). By the end of that year "... it was evident that everybody had spoken from whom ideas or words were apt to come, had indicated what he might or might not contribute to the solution. Or rather, all except one" (Miller 1953, 485). That one was Jonathan Edwards.

What Edwards had to offer New England was, first of all, a theology which emphasized the relation of the individual soul to a sovereign God, apart from the complexities of a national covenant (Haroutunian 1932, xxi); second, a spark which ignited the flame of the Great Awakening in America; and finally, a new theoretical framework for comprehending the process and nature of conversion.

It is true that Edwards was not the first pastor in America to experience the power of revival. In the parish of Edwards' father "... there had been 'four or five seasons of the pouring out of the Spirit' since 1694," and Northampton experienced five "harvests" under Solomon Stoddard beginning about 1680 and continuing through 1719 (Gaustad 1957, 17-20). However, none of these was destined to become as influential as the quickening that occurred in 1734-35 under Edwards. In addition, although he paid careful and proper respect to the work of his venerable predecessor, Edwards occasionally hinted "... that Northampton's people, for all their familiarity with revivals, had imbibed a quite mistaken notion of conversion" (Goen in Edwards 1972, 5).

Edwards was genuinely surprised by the work of God in his own congregation, and even more by its spread through many communities in the Connecticut River Valley. "Nothing like it had ever occurred before in New England, where previous revivals were largely sporadic and isolated instances which Edwards suspected of resting too often on an implicit Arminianism" (Goen in Edwards 1972, 25). What gave this revival an even greater significance was the impact which his report of it was destined to have. Edwards' correspondence regarding the revival produced an almost immediate request for fuller details. In response, he penned *A Faithful Narrative of the Surprising Work of God in the Conversion of Many Hundred Souls....* An abridgment was published by Benjamin Colman in Boston in November 1736. The *Narrative* itself was published with some alterations in London in 1737 and in Boston (corrected by Edwards) in 1738 (Goen in Edwards 1972, 32-39).

The *Narrative* immediately established Edwards' international reputation. Interest in England and Scotland was very high, and Edwards developed a regular correspondence with several Scottish ministers. Some of the repercussions of these transatlantic connections will be examined in detail below. For now, it is enough to note that the *Narrative* became a crucial factor in preparing the way for the greater moving of the Spirit in 1740. At least, that was the opinion of Edwards' contemporary, Thomas Prince, minister at Boston's Old South Church, and his evaluation has generally been accepted by students of the revival (Goen in Edwards 1972, 27; Winslow [1940] 1979, 166). Indeed, a number of localized revivals had begun before Whitefield arrived in America, and the increasing concern of pastors and people over their spiritual deadness seems to have owed a great deal to the "surprising conversions" in the Connecticut River Valley (Tracy 11845] 1969, 18-35, 83-84). One aspect of Edwards' *Narrative* was destined to plague him for years to come, that is, the sensational experiences reported by some of his converts. Abigail Hutchinson and Phebe Bartlet, the two examples he chose to exhibit as specimens of the revival both experienced highly emotional conversions. Later, when the enthusiastic extremes of the Great Awakening brought reproach on the whole movement, Edwards' earliest revival piece was partly to blame (Goen in Edwards 1972, 30; Winslow [1940] 1979, 167). Even more significant, at least for the purpose of this study, is the fact that some of the converts actually claimed to have seen visions:

> I do not suppose that they themselves imagined they saw any thing with their bodily eyes; but only have had within them ideas strongly impressed, and as it were lively pictures in their minds: as for instance, some when in great terrors, through fear of hell, have had lively ideas of a dreadful furnace. Some, when their hearts have been strongly impressed, and their affections greatly moved with a sense of the beauty and excellency of Christ, it has wrought on their imaginations so, that together with a sense of his glorious spiritual perfections, there has arisen in the mind an idea of one of glorious majesty, and of a sweet and gracious aspect. Some, when they have been greatly affected with Christ's death, have at the same time a lively idea of Christ hanging upon the cross, and his blood running from his wounds; which things won't be wondered at by them that have observed how strong affections about temporal matters will excite lively ideas and pictures of different things in the mind (Edwards 1972, 188-189).

Fulfillment with a Vengeance

The Great Awakening in New England is generally reckoned to have begun with Whitefield's whirlwind tour through the colonies in the fall of 1740, but isolated examples of quickening actually occurred in 1739. Mr. Secomb, minister at Harvard, reported that "... this religious concern began a year before Mr Whitefield's coming into the country: and after he preached in New England very few of this people did ever hear him. But God was pleased to make use of the usual means, to rouse and awaken sleepy sinners..." (Gillies [1845] 1981, 342). The "usual means" were not to continue as the norm for long, but small beginnings such as this indicate the prepared soil which awaited the famous evangelist when he stepped ashore at Newport, Rhode Island, on September 14. Expectation of a spiritual harvest was high, and New England was not to be disappointed (Tracy [1845] 1969, 83).

From the very beginning, Whitefield drew immense crowds. *The Boston Weekly News Letter* reported audiences of 5,000 and 8,000. By the time Whitefield "... passed from Connecticut into New York, his journal showed that he had spent 45 days, visited 40 towns, and delivered 97 sermons and exhortations." Never had New England been stirred so deeply. The hunger for preaching seemed insatiable; churches were filled with searching souls, and pastors reported an astonishing number of inquirers. Convinced that New England was ready for harvesting, Whitefield persuaded New Jersey evangelist, Gilbert Tennent, to "... set out for Boston, in order to blow up the divine fire lately kindled there" (Goen in Edwards 1972, 48-50).

For three months Tennent thundered at the people, and heavenly fire fell in abundance. These were the glorious days of the revival. In 1741 many of the clergy encouraged the itinerants, and those who did not were at least willing to postpone judgment. Charles Chauncy, soon to become the arch-enemy of the Awakening, preached and published *The New Creature Described and Considered...* in which he treated the recent converts as probably genuine, but offered comfort to Christians whose experience of conversion had not been remarkable. The discourse concluded with an exhortation to those who had tasted the heavenly gifts in a greater measure:

> Take care to keep your *zeal* under the government of *sound judgment*. None (commonly) [are] more zealous than *young converts*; and yet none [are] more apt to be carried away with a zeal without knowledge (Chauncy 1741, 39).

It was the mildest rebuke of the revival he was ever to administer.

Ominous signs soon began to show on the horizon. The epithet generally used to encompass most of the irregularities was "enthusiasm." In *Enthusiasm Described and Caution'd Against...* Chauncy discusses the etymology of the word, and then gives its more common usage:

> But the word is more commonly used in a bad sense, as intending to an *imaginary*, not a *real* inspiration: according to which sense, the *Enthusiast* is one, who has a conceit of himself as a person favored with the extraordinary presence of the *Deity*. He mistakes the workings of his own passions for divine communications, and fancies himself immediately inspired by the SPIRIT of GOD, when all the while, he is under no other influence than of an over-heated imagination (Chauncy 1742a, 3).

During the seventeen forties, no charge against the Awakening was so potentially damaging as the accusation that the ecstasies of the converts were the result of enthusiasm. And that became an increasingly easy charge to maintain.

Under the early preaching of Whitefield and Tennent, the people were generally well behaved, and complaints of enthusiasm were few. Thomas Prince of Boston recollected no "... crying out, or falling down, or fainting, either under Mr Whitefield's or Mr Tennent's ministry all the while they were here..." (Gillies [1845] 1981, 351). However, "... such traveling preachers as Wheelock, Buell, Bliss, and Pomeroy soon led the people to expect groans and tears as signs of true remorse. From here it was an easy step to fainting and apparitions." "'Visions and trances'... [became] common during the summer preaching of 1741" (Griffin 1980, 63). Heaven seemed very near to earth in those days, perhaps too near.

The prospect of immediate and infallible communion with God has always been attractive to certain kinds of temperaments, but few have been more powerfully captivated by the idea than James Davenport. From the summer of 1741 through March, 1743, he raged back and forth across New England, wreaking spiritual havoc wherever he went. His story has frequently been told and need not be repeated here (Tracy [1845] 1969, 230-255; Gaustad 1957, 37-41). A brief catalogue of errors will suffice:

> Brockway lists the following eleven distinctive points in Davenport's religious position: (1) continuity of prophetic revelation; (2) ultimate authority of inner experience; (3) divine origin of visions and dreams; (4) symbolic nature of scripture; (5) violent, dramatic conversion experience; (6) no sin after conversion; (7) public exposure and condemnation of unconverted clergy men; (8) absolute necessity of a converted clergy; (9) immediate, intuitive recognition of one converted Christian by another; (10) separation of converts from established churches; and (11) imminence of the judgment (unpublished doctoral dissertation of Robert W. Brockway, cited by Jones 1958, 282).

Visions and dreams, specifically of the person of Christ, will occupy much of this present paper, but in order to capture the atmosphere of those trying times, it may be asked how "violent" and how "dramatic" conversions were expected to be. *The Boston Weekly Post-Boy* offered this (perhaps not unbiased) account of meetings held by the itinerant preachers.

[The terrible language of the itinerants] frequently frights the *little Children*, and sets them a Screaming; and that frights their *tender Mothers*, and sets them to Screaming, and by Degrees spreads over a great Part of the Congregation; And 40, 50, or an 100, of them screaming all together, makes such an awful and hideous Noise as will make a Man's Hair stand an End. Some will faint away, fall down upon the Floor, wallow and foam. Some Women will rend off their Caps, Handkerchiefs, and other Clothes, tear their Hair down about their Ears, and seem perfectly bereft of their Reason (Chauncy [1743] 1975, 106).

Such indecorous behavior could not go long unopposed. 1742, which saw the height of Davenport's madness, also witnessed the beginning of organized and violent opposition to the revival. By the end of 1743 the Great Awakening had come to a halt. While the tempest was raging, no one knew how long the storm would last, how deep the waters would become, or how far reaching the flood damage would be. After it was over, participants on both sides offered their estimates of the situation, but in many cases the facts are difficult to ascertain. Just how widespread was "enthusiasm" during the Awakening? The newspaper account quoted above suggests that its description was typical of the revival meetings, and there is no doubt that outcries and convulsions did become quite common for a time in certain areas. Not all localities were equally affected, however, as contemporary records make clear. Even more obscure is the extent to which the new converts were recipients of visions. The evidence for that is summarized in the next section.

The Extent of the Flood

Many ministers were acquainted with their own localities, but few had the time or inclination to survey the effects of the revival over a larger area. One of the exceptions was Charles Chauncy.

> As for Facts, I have related none but such as I really believe my self, and, as I think, upon sufficient Evidence. Few, perhaps, have taken more pains to inform themselves than I have done. I have been a Circle of more than three hundred Miles, and had, by this Means, an Opportunity of going thro' a great Number of Towns in this, and the neighbouring Government of CONNECTICUT, and of having personal Conversation with most of the Ministers, and many other Gentlemen, in the Country, and of settling a Correspondence with several of them, with a particular View to know, as nearly as might be, the Truth of Things, upon better Evidence than that of meer Hear-say (Chauncy [1743] 1975, xxix, original italicized).

Seasonable Thoughts on the state of Religion in New England was the result.

Unfortunately, Chauncy could only present a selection of the material which he compiled, and visions or trances were not high on his priority list. Although he frequently mentions them as aspects of enthusiasm, Chauncy provides no indication of the numbers of people who experienced visions, nor of the geographical extent of such manifestations, in 424 pages (plus front matter) he gives only one detailed account of such an experience, which occurred after James Davenport left New Haven (Chauncy [1743] 1975, 128-9). Two young women became "exceedingly filled with zeal" at a prayer meeting and were "in some degree depriv'd of their bodily strength." They exhorted those who were present, particularly those they supposed to be unconverted. The next evening, they were so overcome "... that they fell down unable to walk, and so continued, for some Time, lying in the Street like Persons dead or asleep." They were brought into a nearby house where they continued for some time in a state of ecstasy, delivering supposed revelations and messages to a number of people who came to see them. They claimed,

... that they had been to Heaven, had seen the Book of Life, the Names of many Persons of their Acquaintance wrote in it; that they had seen the Seats of the Blessed, and their own Seats empty, and the like.

A few striking examples of visionary experiences are available from other sources. For example, the diary of Jacob Eliot provides the following:

Noah Chappel & Mary Webster aet about 12 were at Night both in a kind of trance & so remained for near 2 Days 2 Nights sometimes .... Screaming & Lamenting—calm and still, with their eyes open seeming as if they were writing or reading as they lay together on a bed they kept one spot between 'em peculiar to 'em; that if but a hair or mote was dropt there they would instantly take it away tho both blinded. They both pretended to be going to heaven ... & ... they had several conflicts with the Devil & that they had a vision of Christ & read in the book of Life in the Golden Capitals several names. Mr. Whitefield's first, then Mr. Wheelocks, Mr. Pomeroy's, Mr. Rogers, Mr. Warren (Griffin 1980, 66).

The manuscript biography, "The Spiritual Travels of Nathan Cole," contains another frequently cited example of a dramatic encounter with God. Cole was the happy recipient of visions from the time of his conversion until the later years of his life. After hearing Whitefield, he came under a spiritual distress which lasted a full year. His anxiety was finally relieved by the words of Christ in the fifteenth chapter of John. Assurance of salvation, however, had to wait for another vision:

It seemed as if I really saw the gate of heaven by an Eye of faith, & the way for Sinners to Get to heaven by Jesus Christ; as plain as ever I saw anything with my bodily eyes in my life... I saw what free Grace was; I saw how stubborn & willfull man was; I saw it was nothing but accepting of Christs Righteousness & the match was made; I saw I was saved by Christ, I thought here I had the sealings of the Holy Ghost; & here I had evidences clear. What I saw here is unspeakable, I could do no work

here but lay down for want of bodily Strength untill this
view was a little abated (Goen 1962, 138).

In this passage, there appears to be an interesting shift in
the object of Cole's sight. At first, he speaks as though he were
seeing a vision, as if some image were present in his mind, but a
sight of "free Grace" is obviously a different matter. Was the
whole experience simply a quickening of his understanding, or
did Cole inadvertently introduce confusion by using the faculty
of sight in a double sense? The latter seems most probable.
First of all (as Jonathan Edwards noted), preachers often spoke
of conversion as "... seeing Christ in His glory ..." and the
common people can hardly be blamed for taking this rather
more literally than was intended (Edwards 1959, 212-13). In the
second place, other passages from Cole's autobiography leave
no doubt that actual images were at times present in his mind.

> At the time of his conversion, Cole had seen in a vision
> 'the form of a Gospel Church, and the place where it was
> settled, and Angels hovering over it, saying, the Glory of
> the town, & strangers that came pressing by had the same
> to say.' He saw exactly the form of the house, the place
> where it stood, the minister who dwelt there, the people
> who worshiped there—all the details are described. When
> Cole later saw the meetinghouse of the Separates in
> Middleton, exactly according to the details of his vision
> (even with the angels hovering over it), he knew he had
> found the pure and true gospel church (Goen 1962, 141).

It is indeed unfortunate for the cause of supernaturalism that
the vision was not recorded until twenty years after its
occurrence, when Cole was already active in the church at
Middleton.

Apart from isolated accounts of visionary experiences, one
of the most fruitful sources of information is *The Christian
History, Containing Accounts of the Revival and Propagation
of Religion in Great Britain & America....* Edited by Thomas
Prince, Jr., this was the first magazine devoted to religious

news in America (Goen in Edwards 1972, 78). It appeared in two volumes and 104 numbers between March, 1743, and February, 1745 (Evans [1904] 1941, 273). The bulk of the material is in the form of letters solicited by Prince. The large number of respondents affords a fairly wide exposure to the reaction of various localities during the Awakening. Unfortunately, many of the accounts follow an almost stereotyped format, and often names or other particulars are suppressed. In addition, the purpose of the magazine was to exhibit the work of God in the extraordinary events of the preceding years—a purpose which discouraged inclusion of very much that would be prejudicial to the revival. And visions were frequently considered to be bad news.

In fact, one of the noteworthy features of the *Christian History* is the obvious relief with which several pastors report that their churches had been free of extravagances. The ministers in Wrentham, Massachusetts, assert, "We have not known *Trances, Visions, Revelations*, or the like. We have had *great freedom* from the appearances of a *censorious Spirit....*" (Prince 1743-5, 1:248). Or consider this from Bridgewater, Massachusetts:

> As to *Antinomianism* and *enthusiastical Frensies*; there are little or no Appearances among us. Indeed, there is that among us that an *Arminian* would account *Antinomianism*, and one that never felt the Power of divine Grace on his own Heart, would account *Enthusiasm*. But this don't make it so. As far as I am capable of judging, their *Principles* and *Practices* are *scriptural*. God grant I may never have the melancholy Occasion to think or say otherwise.
>
> As to *Trances, Visions, &c.*, we have none, and I think have had none from the beginning (Prince 1743-45, 1:407).

One further example of this sort will suffice. It comes from the Rev. Benjamin Bradstreet of Gloucester, Massachusetts.

"Thanks be to God, we have *no Divisions, nor Separations* among us; *we are without Dreams, Visions and Trances,* (though there have been some in the Neighbourhood,) *nor are we troubled with Exhorters*" (Prince 1743-45, 1:188).

Contributors to the Christian History are frequently careful to note their own diligence in discouraging enthusiasm. John White, pastor of another parish in Gloucester asserts:

> As to *Visions* we had enough of them, until such *Time* as in a Lecture Sermon I declared my Sentiments concerning them; and so far as I can understand, there has never been one since. Our Congregation has been disturbed and interrupted by *Outcries*, but I laboured to suppress them (Prince 1743-45, 2:45).

White's lecture must have been uncommonly effective. Sometimes the incursions of fanaticism were much deeper. Itinerant preacher, Eleazer Wheelock, records in his private journal the aberrations at Voluntown:

> There is a great work in this town; but more of the footsteps of Satan than in any place I have yet been in: the zeal of some too furious: they tell of many visions, revelations, and many strong impressions upon the imagination. They have had much of God in their meetings, and his great power has been much seen, and many hopefully converted. Satan is using many artful wiles to put a stop to the work of God in this place (Tracy [1845] 1969, 201).

This entry is dated October 21, 1741, some months before the frenzy was at its peak. One of the most interesting accounts provided by the *Christian History* comes from the pen of Jonathan Edwards. In a letter dated December 12, 1743, he describes the progress of the revival in Northampton (Prince 1743-45, 1:367-381; Edwards 1972, 544-557). In the early period of 1740-41 the work seemed to be even more pure than during the outpouring of the Spirit in 1735-36. Heightened concern began in Northampton in the spring of 1740.

Whitefield arrived in the middle of the following October, and
the "professors" to whom he chiefly addressed himself began to
experience revival. Shortly afterwards some of the unsaved
became concerned about their souls, and were apparently
converted. By the spring of 1741 people began to be more visibly
affected during public meetings.

> The Months of *August* and *September* were the most
> remarkable of any *this Year*, for *Appearances* of
> *Conviction* and *Conversion* of *Sinners*, and great
> *Revivings, Quickenings*, and *Comforts* of *Professors*, and
> for extra ordinary external Effects of these Things. It was
> a very *frequent thing* to see an *house full* of *Out-cries,
> Faintings, Convulsions*, and such like, both with *distress,*
> and also with Admiration and *joy*....

> *One Circumstance* wherein this Work differed from
> that which had been in the Town *five* or *six years* before,
> was that Conversions were frequently wrought *more
> sensibly and visibly*; the Impressions stronger, and more
> manifest by external Effects of them; and the Progress of
> the SPIRIT of GOD in Conviction, from Step to Step, more
> apparent; and the Transition from one State to another
> more sensible and plain; so that it might, in many
> Instances, be as it were seen by By-standers. The
> *preceding Season* had been very remarkable on this
> Account beyond what had been before; but *this* more
> remarkable than *that*. And in this Season these apparent
> or visible Conversions (if I may so call them) were more
> frequently in the Presence of others, at religious Meetings,
> where the Appearances of what was wrought on the Heart
> fell under public Observation.

> After *September* 1741, there seemed to be some
> Abatement of the extraordinary Appearances that had
> been; but yet they did not wholly cease, but there was
> something of them from Time to Time *all winter* (Prince
> 1743-5, 1:371-373).

In February of 1742 Mr. Buell came to Northampton during
the absence of Edwards. His ministry was signally blessed in
the stirring up of professors. The work among the unconverted

was considerably less effective than during the summer before. Mr. Buell stayed two or three weeks after Edwards arrived home. Edwards describes what he observed:

> When I came home, I found the Town in very extraordinary Circumstances, such, in some Respects, as I never saw it in before. . . , many in their religious Affections being raised far beyond what they ever had been before; and there were *some instances* of Persons lying in a *sort of Trance*, remaining for perhaps a whole *twenty-four Hours motionless*, and with their Senses locked up; but in the mean Time, under strong Imaginations, as though they went to Heaven, and had there a Vision of glorious and delightful Objects. But when the People were raised to this Height, *Satan* took the advantage, and his Interposition in many instances soon became very apparent; and a great deal of Caution and Pains were found necessary to keep the People, many of them, from running wild (Prince 1743-5, 1:373).

Edwards does not seem to blame the excesses of this period on Buell so much as on the influences of other outsiders. He complains that his people were "infected from abroad" by visitors who "... went far beyond them in Raptures and violent Emotions of the Affections, and a vehement Zeal...." As a consequence, many began to minimize their own experiences of grace and to defer to the bold claims of others. "These Things had a strange Influence on the People, and gave many of them a deep and unhappy Tincture, that it was a hard and long Labour to deliver 'em from, and which some of them are not fully delivered from to this day" (Prince 1743-45, 1:379-80).

Visions there were, and sometimes in sufficient numbers to cause grave concern. However, several considerations suggest that they never became a general or widely expected phenomenon. First of all, many churches had no such experiences at all. Frequently pastors were able effectively to forewarn their people regarding the dangers of enthusiasm.

Second, the testimonies of the pastors frequently included an indication of the scores, or sometimes hundreds, who were apparently converted. The changed lives and godly affections of these new believers was a great cause for joy. Even if some were spurious, most appeared to be genuine. These facts, coupled with the widespread fear of enthusiasm, make it clear that in many parishes visions, the most extreme form of enthusiasm, must not have been a great problem. Finally, when visions did occur the regular clergy normally took measures to curtail their influence and spread. On occasion, such measures were immediately effective, but even when this was not so, the number permanently affected was probably slight. The testimony of the Rev. Jonathan Parsons of the west parish in Lyme, Connecticut, corroborates these conclusions (Prince 1743-45, 2:118-162).

Parsons began his ministry as an "Arminian" but was later led to reject his early principles. The congregation quarreled with his Calvinism and seemed unresponsive to his insistence on a sensible experience of conversion and communion with Christ. Whitefield's arrival in the colonies stirred up a fresh zeal in the pastor for the salvation of his people, and in March, 1741, Parsons went to Hartford to investigate for himself. He returned to Lyme convinced that the revival was indeed a work of God. It was not long after wards that his congregation was visited with an outpouring of the Holy Spirit. Parsons, himself, went on to become an efficient promoter of the revival. His people were for a time affected by the errors of Davenport, but Parsons turned the tide with a sermon, "Needful Caution in a Critical Day," preached on February 4, 1742. Tracy's summary of the situation is significant:

> It had been reported, that "trances, visions, extraordinary missions and immediate revelations" were common among the new converts; but though he was extensively

acquainted with them, and had conversed with thousands of them, he had "not met with a score who pretend to any such thing," and he doubted whether half that number could be found in Connecticut. And yet his acquaintance included the region where they were said to be most abundant (Tracy [1845] 1969, 146).

Apparently, a few individuals and groups in various townships were able to generate an immense amount of publicity and curiosity, but their number never approached anything like the number of those who were affected in other ways. Outcries and convulsions were certainly much more common. "Towards the close of the Great Awakening of 1740, these 'manifestations' began to assume the character of an epidemic. . ." (Tracy [1845] 1969, 223). This, together with the fact that Davenport openly encouraged visions, dreams and trances led conservative pastors to fear the worst, and Charles Chauncy was, in these matters, a most conservative pastor. To his reaction and the response of Jonathan Edwards it is now necessary to turn.

Reaction and Response

Chauncy was not the only opponent of the Awakening. "One of the outstanding treatises produced in the Awakening Period was *An Enquiry Into Enthusiasm* by Benjamin Doolittle of Northfield" (Gaustad 1957, 78). However, Chauncy led the attack. He was probably the most learned, and certainly the most diligent of the anti-revivalists. As he later confided to Ezra Stiles:

> I wrote and printed in that day more than two volumes in octavo. A vast number of pieces were published also as written by others; but there was scarce a piece against the times but was sent to me, and I had the labor sometimes of preparing it for the press, and always of correcting the press (Goen in Edwards 1972, 64).

As the excesses of "enthusiasm" increased, Chauncy*s attitude toward the revival hardened. 1742 saw the publi cation of several sermons and two anonymous pieces. The second of these is of special interest. It was entitled, *The Wonderful Narrative; or, a Faithful Account of the French Prophets, Their Agitations, Extasies, and Inspirations. To Which Are Added, Several Other Remarkable Instances of Persons Under the Influence of the Like Spirit, in Various Parts of the World, Particularly in New England.* It was published in Boston, and Edwards assumed Chauncy was the author. Most scholars have allowed his verdict (Miller [1949] 1973, 203; Goen in Edwards 1972, 63).

The *Wonderful Narrative* was a pretty piece of slander by association. After the revocation of the Edict of Nantes in 1685, the mood of many Huguenots was ripe for some form of apocalyptic prophetism. It was not long in coming. Prophecies were accompanied by convulsions, and even children were trained in the arts of producing a fever pitch in themselves and their auditors. When persecution intensified, the French Prophets fled, primarily to Germany and England where they created quite a stir (Knox 1950, 356-71). Chauncy gives a brief history of these prophets in their homeland, followed by the testimony of three notable English adherents. The "*pretended Inspiration*" of the prophets is next demonstrated to be ". . . wholly a Scene either of *Imposter*, or *Delusion*, or over-heated *Imagination*, or a *Mixture* of them all" ([Chauncy] 1742c, 49). Actually, only one proof is offered, since it is conclusive by itself, that is, the failure of the prophets' predictions to come true. Several of them prophesied the resurrection of one of their leaders, a Dr. Emes. The prediction was published in advance as an expressly stated test of the inspiration of the prophets. On the specified day, May 25, 1708, approximately twenty thousand people showed up to witness the miracle. When Dr.

Emes refused to cooperate, the influence of the sect evaporated ([Chauncy] 1742c, 52-59).

The *Wonderful Narrative* is climaxed by an appendix from the purported recipient of the foregoing letter, a certain "ANTI-ENTHUSIASTICUS," who compares the French Prophets with the present revival. He does not deny that there might be some small mixture of real Christianity in the extraordinary events of the day.

> But if by the *Work of God* any should understand that FALLING DOWN, and SCREAMING OUT, and *SWOONING AWAY*, in the Time of *preaching*, or just after the *Preacher* is gone from the House of Worship; those VISIONS or Representations to the *bodily sight*, of *Christ* and the Devil; Those TRANCES, wherein the Subjects of them have a clear and distinct View of *Heaven* and *Hell*; of the *Process of the last Judgment*; of the *Book of Life*, with the Names of particular Persons wrote there; those extravagant FITS OF LAUGHING; UNCHRISTIAN CENSORIOUSNESS, and the like:... I have no Opinion of them as *Fruits of the Spirit of God*... ([Chauncy] 1742c, 96-7).

The same opinion continued to be expressed in the following year. In 1743 Chauncy published two pieces directed specifically at Jonathan Edwards. Early in the year he published The *Late Religious Commotions in New England. An Answer to the Reverend Mr. Jonathan Edwards's Sermon, Entitled, The Distinguishing Marks of a Work of the Spirit of God....* Later, *Seasonable Thoughts on the State of Religion in New England...* appeared as a response to Edwards' *Some Thoughts concerning the Present Revival of Religion in New England...* (Miller, [1949] 1973, 174-75). In both works the conclusion is the same. If revivalists claim that God is doing an extraordinary work, they must produce proof. But the only extraordinary events are precisely those which give least evidence of a divine origin. Not withstanding the abuses of extremists,

... Mr. Edwards supposes "that the Work *in general* may be the Work of the SPIRIT of GOD." I do not well understand what Mr. Edwards means by the *Work in general*. If he means the *extraordinary* Appearances in those that are supposed to be the Subjects of the Work, such as their *crying out, falling down, bodily Agitations and Convulsive Motions, Swoons, Trances and Visions*: If he means that *these* in general are the Work of God, I confess, I can see *no* Evidence of it. And yet, I think, Mr. *Edwards* must by *the Work in general*, mean *these* Things, or what amounts to much the same, those Impressions upon the Mind from whence *those* Appearances proceed; for I believe these *extraordinary Appearances* are the only, or at least, the *main* Things, from whence Mr. Edwards, and many others, are so very confident, that there is such a glorious Work going on in the Land (Chauncy 1743, 20-21).

These were serious accusations, and they demanded a suitable response. Edwards' defense of the revival is primarily contained in four pieces, three of which have already been noted. They are, his *Narrative of Surprising Conversions* (1737), *Distinguishing Marks of a Work of the Spirit of God* (1741), and *Thoughts concerning the Present Revival of Religion in New England* (1743, cf. Goen in Edwards 1972, 65). The fourth, representing Edwards' mature thoughts on the subject, came after the fires of controversy had begun to cool. *A Treatise concerning Religious Affections* appeared in 1746. An investigation of these and other documents yields two rather surprising conclusions. The first is that the explanation of visionary experiences offered by Edwards has much in common with that given by other ministers of the time, including both opponents and supporters of the revival. The second is that Edwards remained consistent in his attempts to deal with the phenomena. Controversy altered his emphasis, but not his understanding. Both of these assertions require some expansion.

The supporters of James Davenport insisted that visions be recognized as direct communications from God. A few pastors (on both sides of the controversy) regularly ascribed them to demonic delusion. However, most American ministers preferred a naturalistic explanation. In this Edwards did not differ from his contemporaries. The prevailing opinion held that visions and trances were the natural result of extreme excitement in certain types of personalities. Under powerful emotional stimuli the imagination could receive visual impressions that seemed as vivid as actual sight. But what were the nature of those stimuli? Were they divine, demonic, physical or psychological? Chauncy's party was convinced that,

> The cause of this *enthusiasm* is a bad temperament of the blood and spirits; 'tis properly a disease, a sort of madness: And there are few; perhaps, none at all, but are subject to it; tho' none are so much in danger of it as those, in whom *melancholy* is the prevailing ingredient in their constitution (Chauncy 1742a, 3).

Accordingly, James Davenport's career in Connecticut was interrupted when the court in Hartford judged him "disturbed in the rational faculties of his mind" and had him deported (Goen in Edwards 1972, 60).

Edwards laid down his doctrine in a sermon preached at Northampton in August, 1733, before the outpourings of the Spirit had begun to raise questions (Winslow [1940] 1979, 159). It was published a year later. He wrote that the "spiritual and divine light" which accompanies regeneration

> ... is no impression upon the mind, as though one saw any thing with the bodily eyes. It is no imagination or idea of an outward light or glory, or any beauty of form or countenance, or a visible lustre or brightness of any object. The imagination may be strongly impressed with such things; but this is not spiritual light. Indeed when the mind has a lively discovery of spiritual things, and is greatly affected by the power of divine light, it may, and

> probably very commonly doth, much affect the
> imagination; so that impressions of an outward beauty or
> brightness may *accompany* those spiritual discoveries.
> But spiritual light is not that impression upon the
> imagination, but an exceedingly different thing. Natural
> men may have lively impressions on their imaginations;
> and we cannot determine but that the devil, who
> transforms himself into an angel of light, may cause
> imaginations of an outward beauty, or visible glory, and of
> sounds and speeches, and other such things; but these are
> things of a vastly inferior nature to spiritual light
> (Edwards [1834] 1974, 2:13).

Edwards recognized that visions may come from Satan, but as
he reviewed the evidences of genuine grace among his people,
he concluded that such lively impressions on the imagination
could be, and often were, normal accompaniments of a real
sense of divine things.

When he wrote the *Narrative* a few years later, Edwards
neglected to mention the Devil's influence and concentrated
instead on the way in which gracious affections might give rise
to visionary experiences. He also mentioned that there had
been

> ... some few instances of impressions on persons'
> imaginations, which have been something mysterious to
> me, and I have been at a loss about them.... I have not
> been able well to satisfy myself, whether their imaginary
> ideas have been more than could naturally arise from
> their spiritual sense of things (Edwards 1972, 189).

It was an unfortunate admission, and although Edwards
insisted that no one trust in such imaginary ideas of Christ, the
damage had been done. *Distinguishing Marks* continued the
discussion in the same vein.

> Some persons are ready to interpret such things wrong,
> and to lay too much weight on them, as prophetical
> visions, and to look upon what they imagine they see or
> hear in them as divine revelations, and sometimes
> significations from heaven of what shall come to pass;

which the issue, in some instances I have known, has shown to be otherwise: but yet, it appears to me that such things are evidently sometimes from the Spirit of God, though indirectly; that is, as that extraordinary frame of mind they are in, and that strong and lively sense of divine things that is the occasion of them, is from his Spirit; and also as the mind continues in its holy frame, and retains a divine sense of the excellency of spiritual things, even in its rapture: which holy frame and sense is from the Spirit of God, though the_ imaginations that attend it are but accidental, and therefore there is commonly something or other in them that is confused, improper and false (Edwards 1972, 237-38).

When Edwards published his *Thoughts concerning the Present Revival* the emphasis was still the same. Although imagination is a natural faculty and its strength is often dependent on the constitution of the body, nevertheless, impressions on the imagination can be of great benefit to godly persons. Outcries and faintings of those under conviction are at least probable indications of God's presence (Edwards [1834] 1981, 1: 394, 411).

Time passed, and Edwards realized his doctrine of regeneration required a more thorough defense than he had yet given. The result, *A Treatise concerning Religious Affections*, is a careful attempt at discriminating between true and false conversion. There is no change in his central tenets, but the emphasis has shifted. Visions are not different from external ideas which may be present in all men; they are essentially neutral in their religious significance, since they may accompany either gracious or spurious affections. However, in this work Edwards has very little to say for the positive value of such impressions on the imagination. Since his aim is to distinguish a truly spiritual sense of the excellencies of Christ from imitations, he carefully prunes away all experiences which may occur to an unsaved man. His examples are all of the manner in which men may be deceived by visions into believing that they are regenerate.

> Let us suppose a person who has been for some time in great exercise and terror through fear of hell, and his heart weakened with distress and dreadful apprehensions, and upon the brink of despair, and is all at once delivered, by being firmly made to believe, through some delusion of Satan, that God has pardoned him... as suppose through some vision, or strong idea or imagination, suddenly excited in him, of a person with a beautiful countenance, smiling on him, with arms open, and with blood dropping down, which the person conceives to be Christ, without any other enlightening of the understanding to give a view of the spiritual, divine excellency of Christ and his fullness.... It is easy to be accounted for, from the principles of nature, that a person's heart, on such an occasion, should be raised up to the skies with transports of joy, and be filled with fervent affection to that imaginary God or Redeemer... (Edwards 1959, 159).

Again, he writes:

> Many who have had such things have very ignorantly supposed them to be of the nature of spiritual discoveries. They have had lively ideas of some external shape, and beautiful form of countenance; and this they call spiritually seeing Christ. Some have had impressed upon them ideas of a great outward light; and this they call a spiritual discovery of God's or Christ's glory. Some have had ideas of Christ's hanging on the cross, and his blood running from his wounds; and this they call a spiritual sight of Christ crucified, and the way of salvation by his blood. Some have seen him with his arms open ready to embrace them; and this they call a discovery of the sufficiency of Christ's grace and love. Some have had lively ideas of heaven, and of Christ on his throne there, and shining ranks of saints and angels; and this they call seeing heaven opened to them. Some from time to time have had a lively idea of a person of a beautiful countenance smiling upon them; and this they call a spiritual discovery of the love of Christ to their souls, and

tasting the love of Christ. And they look upon it as
sufficient evidence that these things are spiritual
discoveries, and that they see them spiritually, because
they say they don't see these things with their bodily eyes,
but in their hearts; for they can see them when their eyes
are shut (Edwards 1959, 211-12).

As a matter of fact, a vision of Christ hanging on the cross is
not essentially different than seeing Him in the flesh, and that
was possible for even his enemies, the Jews, who watched his
crucifixion (Edwards 1959, 214). To a modern mind, it may
seem strange that Edwards could assert the essential identity of
a mental image of Christ with a physical sight of Him. However,
for Edwards it was a commonplace conclusion drawn from the
psychology of the day. That psychology has a fascination of its
own, but its relationship to visions must wait until a later
chapter. In the meanwhile, it is necessary to look across the sea
at some unexpected repercussions of Edwards' teaching on an
"imaginary idea" of Christ.

In 1742 editions of *Distinguishing Marks* appeared in
London, Edinburgh and Glasgow (Goen in Edwards 1972, 60).
Revival and its attendant controversies had already begun in
the west of Scotland, and the pastor of Northampton found a
ready audience. The arrival of *Distinguishing Marks* was
destined to add a new dimension to the conflict.

The Lamentable State of the Church

Scotland was a nation pledged to God, one people bound up in a covenant with the Lord and His true Kirk. That was the theory, but during the early seventeenth century reality was becoming increasingly reluctant to conform. After the Glorious Revolution, the crown made a concerted effort to unify the church in Scotland. Except for a few Cameronians who refused to submit, most of the people were included under the aegis of the national church. So were most of the ministers. And there was the rub. Alongside doughty defenders of Presbyterianism stood the remnants of episcopacy. Marked more by political acumen than by spiritual vigor these former priests began to exert an increasing influence in the General Assembly. Gradually, godly ministers were edged into positions of lesser influence and responsibility. The church began to drift toward the reasonable religion which engulfed Europe during the Enlightenment. "In Scotland there was the rise of Moderatism, stressing the religion of taste and feeling, the cult of Good Manners, of, first and last, polish. Presbyterianism had to be shown as a religion fit for gentlemen" (Fawcett 1971, 2).

That the Age of Reason did not complete its triumph in Scotland may be partly due to the influence of Thomas Boston and the *Marrow of Modern Divinity*, a collection of extracts from reformed writers, first published in London in 1645. Boston, though a minister, was dissatisfied with his spiritual experience. His rediscovery of the *Marrow* introduced many in Scotland to evangelical zeal and the free offer of the Gospel. Opposition to the *Marrow* was intense, and in 1720 the General Assembly condemned the work and forbade ministers to recommend or print it. The resulting controversy rocked the church (Lachman 1979). "The Marrow Men trembled on the very brink of secession, but that step was made incredibly difficult by the historic assertion that there was but one kirk in Scotland" (Fawcett 1971, 23).

Difficult days followed in which, time after time, the General Assembly prevented the settlement of evangelical ministers in local charges. Matters came to a head in 1731 with the passage of an Act giving patrons the sole right of electing ministers for their parishes. This was objection able on two grounds. First, it removed the right of the congregation to reject a minister not of their liking. Second, many of the heritors were unconverted, and the men they presented to the churches were frequently of the same stamp. Ebenezer Erskine, a supporter of the *Marrow*, took up the challenge, and in 1733 he and three other ministers were suspended from the ministry. In December of that year they voted to constitute themselves into a Presbytery. Thus, the Associate Presbytery of the Secession Church was founded with four members, Ebenezer Erskine, William Wilson, Alexander Moncrieff, and James Fisher. After much hesitation and soul searching they were joined by Ebenezer's brother Ralph in 1737 (MacEwen 1900, 63-95; Fraser 1834, 211-214). Initially, relations between members of the Secession Church and evangelical ministers of the established church were cordial, but in the coming days of revival that was destined to change.

The Secession ministers were blessed by God. Their work prospered, and new churches were added even more quickly than ministers could be trained to meet the demand. The evangelistic preaching of the Associate Presbytery attracted attention from evangelicals outside of Scotland, and Ralph Erskine became a frequent correspondent of George Whitefield (Fraser 1834, 297-324). The affection that is everywhere apparent in their letters ended abruptly, however, when Whitefield came to Scotland in the summer of 1741.

The Erskines plainly expected that Whitefield's preaching would strengthen the cause of the Associate Presbytery. During their correspondence, he had showed a mild and teachable spirit, and they hoped to be able to persuade him to forsake the errors of episcopacy and join their party. Ralph Erskine wrote in April, 1741:

> Such is the situation of affairs among us, that unless you come with a design to meet and abide with us particularly of the Associate Presbytery, and to make your public appearances in the places especially of their concern,—I would dread the consequences of your coming, lest it should seem equally to countenance our persecutors. Your fame would occasion a flocking to you, to whatever side you turn; and if it should be in their pulpits, as no doubt some of them would urge, we know not how it would be improved against us (Tracy [1845] 1969, 263).

The desires of the Erskines were not to be fulfilled.

When Whitefield arrived at Leith, July 30, 1741, he went first to preach for Ralph Erskine at Dunfermline. The message was warmly received, and Ralph wrote an encouraging letter to his brother Ebenezer. Within a few days, however, all was changed. The Associate Presbytery gathered with the express purpose of dealing with Whitefield's views on church polity. To their dismay, Whitefield's catholic spirit refused to be confined within the narrow borders prescribed by any sect of Christendom. It was bad enough that the evangelist showed no interest in subscribing to the Solemn League and Covenant, but then he reiterated his conviction that Scripture allows for differing forms of church government. Even worse, he refused to preach exclusively for congregations of the Secession Church. The breach which resulted was sudden, irreversible, and filled with acrimony (Fraser 1834, 325- 344). If matters had been left to the Erskines, perhaps the wounds could have been healed, but there were hotter heads than theirs on the council (MacEwen 1900, 120). Later on, the Associate Presbytery attempted to minimize or deny the part their members had played in bringing Whitefield to Scotland (Fisher 1743, 65-66).

Rejected by the Seceders, Whitefield received a warm welcome from evangelical pastors of the Established Church. The moderates were not so well pleased, but few dared to treat him rudely, at least at first. He preached at Edinburgh for several weeks and then began a tour of the Scottish provinces. At Glasgow he preached ten times with good results. Among those present at Glasgow were at least fourteen people who became subjects of the revival in nearby Cambuslang a few months later (Fawcett 1971, 102-3). To that revival it is now time to turn.

New England Speaks—Scotland Replies

The minister at Cambuslang, William M'Culloch, was not a dynamic preacher. His son describes him as "Thoughtful and studious," but not eloquent; "...his manner was slow and cautious—very different from that of popular orators" " (MacFarlan n.d., 35). Another supporter of the revival described him as "...a Gentleman of *known Piety* and *Learning*, [who] has but a weak voice, no violent Action, and is far from endeavouring to stir up unreasonable Passions..." (Webster 1742a, 15). However, he did have a great concern for the souls of his people. Edwards' *Narrative* had stirred up keen interest in Scotland (Goen in Edwards 1972, 40), and when Whitefield began to minister with great success in England and America, pious souls in Scotland began to long for a taste of the same spiritual refreshing. In the winter of 1741 M'Culloch's preaching began to take on a new emphasis.

> The minister of that parish, in his ordinary course of
> sermons, for near a twelvemonth before this work began,

had been preaching on these subjects which tend most directly to explain the nature, and prove the necessity of regeneration, according to the different lights in which that important matter is represented in holy scripture: and for some months before the late remarkable events, a more than ordinary concern about religion appeared among that people... (Robe 1790, 2).

James Robe of Kilsyth, who became a leading figure in the revival, was impressed with the spiritual deadness of his people and began preaching on the same subject even earlier, in 1740 (Robe 1790, 68).

Perhaps even more significantly, M'Culloch began passing on news of the revival in England and America to his congregation.

On Sabbath evenings after the sermon, he 'frequently read to his hearers, missives, attestations and journals which he had received from his correspondents, giving an account of conversions which had taken place in different parts of the world, especially in New England under Mr Whitefield's ministry' (Fawcett 1971, 97-98).

His congregation was ripe for the harvest when Whitefield came to reap, but the revival did not actually break out until three and a half months after the famous evangelist had left. M'Culloch's messages began to bear fruit, and several individuals came to him in "... deep concern about their salvation, yet there came no great numbers together." Finally, on February 18, 1742, after the weekday sermon "... a considerable number of people, reckoned by some present about fifty, came together to the minister's house, under convictions and alarming apprehensions about the state of their souls..." (Robe 1790, 3).

After this the revival spread rapidly, especially in the parishes around Glasgow, although there is an attestation of the work from Golspie in one of the two northernmost counties on the mainland of Scotland (MacFarlan n.d., 254). Some details of that report are of interest since they provide further evidence of the close connections between Scotland and New England. The minister of Golspie had laboured for several years with little apparent fruit.

> In this uncomfortable state of things, and amidst my greater fears than hopes, I took care to notify to the people the blessed and wonderful success of the Gospel in the British colonies of America, so soon as I had certain accounts of it, by the printed declarations of Messrs Edwards and Cooper, and others (Gillies [1845] 1981, 456).

News of God's mercy at Cambuslang provided further stimulation, but revival did not sweep through the parish until 1744.

When Whitefield returned to Scotland in June, 1742, the work was progressing well, and he was able to participate in two memorable communion services. Both services were held in the fields on a hillside near Cambuslang. At the first, on July 11, the congregation was estimated between twenty and thirty thousand. Approximately seventeen hundred communicated. Because of the remarkable blessing at that season, an unprecedented second communion was held on August 15. The crowds were enormous. Estimates ranged between thirty and fifty thousand, with about three thousand communicants. By comparison, the population of Glasgow in 1740 was only 17,034 (Fawcett 1971, 115-119). Although Whitefield was not present when the revival began, "His first coming to the west of Scotland in the summer of 1741 provided a much-valued inspiration, and his second visit in the following summer proved an irresistible magnet for the multitudes" (Fawcett 1971, 113). This was the high point of the revival.

Fortunately, the stirring events of those days were carefully chronicled by the chief participants. Whitefield's journals are well known, of course, but James Robe and William M'Culloch also took special care to preserve records of the revival. Even before the remarkable conversions began at Cambuslang, M'Culloch began editing *The Weekly History*, a paper of eight pages reporting revival news, at first from other countries, then from Scotland. It began in December 1741 and ran for fifty-two issues. Shortly after it ceased, Robe introduced the *Christian Monthly History*, which began in November 1743 and continued for two years. Both papers served to report, promote, and defend the revival. In May, 1742, *A Short Narrative of the Extraordinary Work of the Spirit of God, at Cambuslang; in a Letter to a Friend. With Attestations...* was published. Later on that year James Robe detailed the events in his parish in *A Faithful Narrative of the Extraordinary work of the Spirit of God, at Kilsyth....* (Later editions combined these two works with several subsequent attestations to the enduring nature of the conversions.) In addition, two manuscript volumes are preserved containing case histories collected by M'Culloch. They relate the conversion experiences of a hundred and five of the persevering subjects of the work, and are written mostly in the converts' own words (MacFarlan n.d., 105-6).

The literary activity of the revival preachers could not help but interest like-minded men on the other side of the Atlantic, and a lively correspondence developed between Jonathan Edwards and several of them. Among these were "... the Rev. William M'Culloch of Cambuslang, the Rev. John [sic, James] Robe of Kilsyth, the Rev. John M'Laurin of Glasgow, the Rev. Thomas Gillespie of Carnoch, the Rev. oJohn Willison of Dundee, and the Rev. John Erskine of Kirkintilloch..." (Edwards [1834] 1974, l:lxxii). The importance of these connections for the present study is the witness they bear to the essential identity of Edwards' sentiments with those of the Scottish revivalists. Visionary experiences were to become a central factor in the revival controversy in Scotland, and

Edwards' views were of considerable importance. In March, 1744, he wrote to reassure M'Culloch on that score:

> You inquire of me, Rev. Sir, whether I reject all those for counterfeits that speak of visions and trances. I am far from doing of it: I am and always have been, in that matter, of the same opinion that Mr. Robe expresses, in some of those pamphlets Mr. M'Laurin sent me, that persons are neither to be rejected nor approved on such a foundation. I have expressed the same thing in my discourse on *The Marks of a Work of the True Spirit*, and han't changed my mind (Edwards 1972, 560).

Visions and trances were matters of concern in Scotland as well as in America. Some of the converts had experienced them, and opponents of the revival eagerly seized upon such accounts to discredit the whole movement. According to one anonymous gentleman:

> THERE are some who tax them with Delusion; nor do I well see how they can clear themselves of that Imputation; for besides the Things mentioned above, a Woman who had been formerly a Seceder, declared openly before Mr. *Fisher* and his Elders, that she had seen Christ with her bodily Eyes, and another of them, *R----t* B-------'s Wife, would not take her Child to Bed with her, because says she, *It stinks of Sin*; but afterwards the Child having vomit up some ugly Stuff, which the Mother said was *original Sin*, she very kindly received *Her dear converted Baby* (Gentleman 1742, 11-12).

Before examining the attacks on the revival, it is helpful to inquire into the extent of these and other manifestations of "enthusiasm" in the Cambuslang work.

Clamor in the Kirk

Great upheavals of the emotions are common in periods of revival. As on the day of Pentecost, hearts are pricked, and men cry out "... what shall we do?" (Acts 2:37). James Robe became active in the Cambuslang work some weeks before there was any indication of quickening in his own congregation. There were a few instances of people falling under spiritual distress in the early spring of 1742, but the first outbreak of mass concern occurred on May 16.

> An extraordinary power of the Spirit from on high accompanied the word preached. There was a great mourning in the congregation.... After the dismission of the congregation, an essay was made to get the distressed into my barn, but it could not be done; the number of them, and of their friends attending them, were so many. I was obliged to convene them in the kirk (Robe 1790, 75).

Robe was not entirely unprepared for emotional outbursts, and he was quite aware that they had already become a source of contention by opponents of the work at Cambuslang. He therefore determined to deal firmly with his own congregation.

> ... when I heard these outcries, and saw the bodily distresses some of the awakened were under, it proved at first very uneasy to me, it appeared unpleasant, yea even shocking; I therefore resolved, that as soon as any fell under remarkable distress, they should be carried out of the congregation, into a separate place I had provided for them, and appointed some of the elders to carry them off accordingly. I also prayed, that if it were the holy will of God, he would bring them to a sight of their sin and danger, without these bodily distresses, which were so unpleasant to behold, so distressing to the people themselves, and offensive to severals. The Lord in a little time discovered unto me my error and imprudence in this. For after I had conversed for sometime with the distressed, I found the distress of their minds to be so great, as they could not but naturally have such effects upon their bodies.... They told me, That they were under dreadful apprehensions of the terrible wrath of God, due to them for their sins, especially for their slighting of Jesus Christ by unbelief. This view made what was before shocking easy to me (Robe 1790, 84-5).

Robe further concluded that it was more disruptive to the services to remove the distressed than to allow them to remain.

In addition, experience proved that God used the visible convictions of some to awaken others who had previously been unconcerned.

In March of 1743 Robe wrote a careful account of the people within his experience who had been subject to unusual bodily manifestations during the revival. There were only two, both "very strong men," who complained of pain in their arms and legs. Trembling was the most common physical expression of distress observed by Robe. In a few cases the agitation was so pronounced that it resulted in convulsions or fainting. These symptoms occurred in three or four men, a half dozen boys, a few women, and several girls. Robe notes that several of these were either "very ignorant" or "of tender and weakly constitutions." in spite of the insinuations of opponents, none of those who were convulsive showed the ordinary symptoms of epilepsy, and there were no examples of foaming at the mouth. This class was very small in comparison with the total number of the awakened. Finally, there were a number of instances of persons who engaged in loud praise or weeping because of their joy in Christ (Robe 1790, 195-200).

Considering the hundreds of people with whom Robe conversed, there seem to have been relatively few who experienced extreme physical effects. However, the figure may be somewhat greater than he suggests when the milder forms are included. In addition, some parishes may not have been as well regulated as his. "It was estimated that these bodily effects did not appear in more than one fifth, some said not more than one eighth, of the awakened. ... As the revival advanced, they became less frequent, and nearly disappeared" (Tracy [1845] 1969, 269).

Robe also undertook a complete listing of those who had reported visions to him.

Under this article, a historical account is to be given of these whose imagination appeared to have been affected. There have been exceeding great misrepresentations of this both here, and elsewhere. The instances of such are very few, and so inconsiderable, that they gave me no manner of uneasiness. Very near the beginning of this work, I instructed the congregation..., That Jesus Christ in the body cannot be seen by any with their bodily eyes in this life.... And therefore if any of them should afterwards think they got any such sights; they would be well persuaded, that it was owing only to the strength of their imagination, to the disorder of their head, and of the humours of their bodies at that time; and that it was not real.... This possibly might be one reason why there was so little of this to be observed here... (Robe 1790, 200).

Robe's statement that there was "so little of this" in Kilsyth may imply that there were parishes in which more cases occurred. However, some congregations were entirely free of them. John Erskine, pastor of Kirkintilloch, writes, "I know nothing of any here having made the least pretensions to visions, dreams, supernatural revelations, &c. And I know not above four or five, whose faith seems founded upon imagination" (Robe 1790, 283).

Robe's most striking account of a vision, and the one to give greatest offense, was related to him by a sick parishioner.

He said, that some days before that, he had been much in earnest and serious prayer or meditation, he thought he saw our Lord Jesus Christ as he hang [sic] upon the cross, the wounds in his hands and feet, and the blood running from his precious wounds. His affections had been greatly moved.... what should he think of it? I instructed him what I could, that he could see no such things by his bodily eyes; that it was owing merely to his being much affected in his thinking upon the death of Jesus Christ; to the strength of his imagination, and to the present bad habit of his body.... It never entered into my mind to assign it to the devil, seeing I could find a sufficient cause for it in the man himself; much less to conclude it inconsistent with a work of grace upon the good man, especially seeing he laid no weight upon it, wanted to be instructed what to judge of it, and readily received instruction. . . (Robe 1790, 201-2).

Robe continues to give a "...faithful history of all I can certainly remember, or have recorded relative to this subject." They are very few. Of the many hundreds he had conversed with, there was one woman who "... thought she saw hell open as a pit to receive her...." A woman and two girls were reported to have seen Jesus, "... but I met with them afterwards, and examined into it, and they appeared to be ashamed of it, and were convinced that they had really seen nothing. And, they did not love to speak of it...." Three other women "... thought they saw a great and glorious light, for a very short time" while their eyes were shut. There were a few instances of individuals who "... had been frightened with the appearance of the devil...." However, Robe is convinced that some of these cases were nothing "... more than some dog that came in their way in the night-time, while they were going to pray, or had been praying in some solitary place." Robe concludes his listing with a young man who heard noises in the roof of his house, and a young woman who was directed in a dream to a text of Scripture with which she had formerly been unacquainted (Robe 1790, 202-204).

Another fruitful source for accounts of visionary experiences is the two volumes of case histories left by William M'Culloch. These have never been published in their entirety. Apparently M'Culloch hoped for their publication, for he had the first volume "... examined by four 'competent judges.' These were Dr. Alexander Webster of Edinburgh; Mr. John Willison of Dundee; Mr. Thomas Gillespie of Carnock; and Mr. James Ogilvie of Aberdeen" (MacFarlan n.d., 109). When MacFarlan printed a selection of these cases, he followed the suggestions of the 'competent judges' and deleted a number of sections. The omissions are significant.

Fawcett, who has examined the manuscript volumes, notes that the four judges regularly excised portions which were suggestive of enthusiasm. Alexander Bilsland coming home from a Monday service

> ...recounted a vision of dead men's bones, similar to that told by the prophet Ezekiel. These turned into "living Men, walking about me.... After which I thought there was a sweet and thick white and soft refreshing shower, falling about me... Manna." Needless to say, all the editors who read the case-histories deleted this story. Margaret Clark in the manse at Cambuslang "verily thought I saw with my bodily eyes, Christ as hanging on the Cross, and a great Light about him in the air." It was a similar testimony to this given by a younger woman, that furnished the Seceders with one of their strongest criticisms of the revival (Fawcett 1971, 149).

Some of the converts were tempted to think that they had received direct communications from heaven and had no further need of the regular ordinances. The gift of prophecy was claimed by a few. However, Scotland lacked a James Davenport and the fire never caught on. Steady opposition to such claims by the leaders of the revival did much to limit the excesses (Fawcett 1971, 149-50). A few of the converts thought they saw the flames of Hell or smelled brimstone from the bottomless pit. But most were moved more by the love of Christ than by threats of damnation (Fawcett 1971, 154-6).

The evidence summarized above suggests that in Scotland, as in New England, visionary experiences were comparatively rare. At least some of the Scottish pastors were careful to preserve records of the aberrant behavior of the minority as well as the more approved experiences of the majority of the converts. However, the more ample case histories of Scotland do not seem to indicate a greater spread of the phenomena.

Before leaving this subject, it may be observed that later evaluations by ministers involved in the revival confirm both the paucity of visionary experiences and the genuineness of a great many of the conversions. Although many became distressed about their souls who never exhibited the abiding fruit of genuine faith, yet a great number of godly people were able to trace their spiritual birth to the revival period. In 1751, the elders of the Kirk at Kilsyth bore witness to the good testimony and Christian conduct of "above a hundred persons" who had been awakened during 1742 and 1743 (Robe 1790, 277). William M'Culloch had, in 1751, a list of over four hundred persevering subjects of the work who had been awakened at Cambuslang. His elders were inclined to think the list too small, but they were able to give personal attestation to the seventy of that number who resided in their parish (Robe 1790, 308, 318).

The passing years also allowed pastors to make invaluable observations on the perseverance of those who were subjects of extraordinary physical or psychological experiences. M'Culloch provides the following insights:

> 3. By all that I can observe or hear, there are more of these that were under deep concern here in 42, that appear still to persevere in a good way, and a gospel-becoming practice, that never cried out aloud in time of public worship; or that were never observably under these bodily agitations above mentioned; than of those that were under such outward commotions, and that made the greatest noise (Robe 1790, 304).

Although many people cried aloud in true repentance for their sins, M'Culloch concludes that some of the extreme manifestations were caused by the Devil.

> When [Satan] saw there was a number here, under deep convictions, and a kindly-like concern about their salvation, that was like to issue well, ... in order to bring disgrace on the work of the Spirit of God, he quickly pitches oh several poor abandoned wretches. . . ; and

teaches some of them, to mimic such as were in soul-distress; causes others of them to cry out publicly, and to fall down as dead for some time, representing various objects to their fancies, in the air, when they were awake, or when asleep, and suggesting various things to their minds at the same time, urging them afterwards to tell what they saw or heard, as visions, dreams, or revelations from heaven; exciting them to go and join in meetings for prayer; and to hold on in this way under a high profession, some for weeks, some for months, and others for years: and then at length to push them into uncleanness, drunkenness, lying, cheating, and all abominations, even to the throwing off (with some) the very profession of religion; which it is to be wished they had never put on (Robe 1790, 307).

As a final conclusion on the matter of visions, the elders of M'Culloch's church at Cambuslang offer the following (1751):

2. Though the most of the subjects of the awakening, whose exercise contained a mixture of strong fancy and imagination, are relapsed to their former sinful courses: yet, there are several instances of persons, whose exercises were mixed with fanciful apprehensions; and which they gave out to be real representations of objects and visions, are of the number of those who are persevering in a justifiable christian profession, and unblemished conversation (Robe 1790, 319).

In 1742, it could not be known how many of the extremists would persevere. Leaders of the revival were persistent even in the early days in discouraging any reliance on visions or voices. However, without denouncing all such effects as demonic they could not satisfy the opposition, and this they were never willing to do. As a matter of fact, even that much of a concession probably would not have helped, other causes of division were already too deep.

Divisions in God's Flock

In New England, the most violent opposition to the Awakening came from a group of men who were to pave the

way for the advent of non-orthodox teaching in the church.
Their quarrel with the revival revealed a temperament
fundamentally at odds with aggressive evangelism. In Scotland
(as among "Old Side" Presbyterians in the Middle Colonies of
America) the case was far different. Sadly, the most virulent
attacks came from the ranks of men devoted to preaching the
truths of the Gospel, the Cameronians and the Secession
Church.

Initially the attacks of the Secession ministers focused on
Whitefield. On June 6, 1742, three days after his arrival at
Leith, Adam Gib launched a vicious attack in a sermon entitled
*A Warning against Countenancing the Ministrations of Mr
George Whitefield*. It was published later that summer with a
preface (dated July 23) and a lengthy appendix

> . . . Wherein are shewn, that Mr. *Whitefield* is *no* Minister
> of *Jesus Christ*; that his *Call* and *Coming* to *Scotland* are
> *scandalous*; that his Practice is *disorderly* and *fertile* of
> Disorder; that his *whole* Doctrine is, and his Success *must*
> be *diabolical*; so that People ought to *avoid* him from
> *Duty* to God, to the Church, to themselves, to Fellow-
> Men, to Posterity, and to *him* (title page).

It is only fair to note that Gib later repented of his
immoderation and "... on his deathbed, wished that there were
no copies of his pamphlet on the face of the earth, and said that
if he could recall every copy, he would burn them" (Tracy
[1845] 1969, 280). (However, I have one.)

The pamphlet is significant because it sounds an early
warning of the coming conflict over visions. The sermon itself
and most of the appendix castigate Whitefield's principle of
tolerating various forms of church government. However, the
sixth and final section deals with the difference between Satan's
action on the imagination and the Holy Spirit's work in the
soul. Since Whitefield leads men to seek a false

. . . Christ, Convictions, Conversions, &c. that are really *Idols*; it is therefore to be fearfully expected, that God will, in Judgment, answer them *accordingly*, and send them an *Idol-Christ, Idol-Conversions, &c.* according to their *Lust* (Gib 1742, 54).

Satan can only work on men's fancies, so his influence is predictable. He carries the imagination away with "... strong, sudden and *blind Impulses, Frights, Freaks, Raptures, Visions, Revelations, Boastings, Blunders...*" (Gib 1742, 58). Gib's prophecies were not simply based on Scripture or on the testimony of prior ages. He had something closer at hand to examine, a pamphlet written in New England, "...transmitted *hither*, reprinted *here*, and warmly recommended by Messieurs *Willison* and W_____d" (Gib 1742, 60). The unnamed tract was *Distinguishing Marks of a Work of the Spirit of God* by Jonathan Edwards.

Adam Gib was not alone in his opinions. During the summer of 1742 the Seceders became convinced that visions were common, and Ralph Erskine preached at least three sermons dealing with the revivals. The first two contain passing references to current events. A "strange work spreading far and near" is recognized to be of the devil since it refuses to acknowledge the genuine work of those who are seeking to restore covenanted religion (Erskine 1865, 3:499-500). Luther and the other Protestant Reformers faced similar opposition from enthusiasts in their day, and modern laborers for reformation must not be surprised if Satan uses the same devices again (Erskine 1865, 3:457). The third sermon, however, openly attacks the new movement and focuses attention on the subject of visions. The title of the sermon, "The True Christ, No New Christ," immediately suggests the theme:

My friends, we live in changeable times, amidst this changeable world. Many, now-a-days, are tempted to change their mind and manners, to change their principles and practice, from better to worse; and the changes amongst many ministers and professors are very strange and alarming.

....

The view of Christ, and his truth, as immutably the same, is needful, in such a season, for shewing the falsehood and damnable tendency of new and strange doctrine; for if God, and Christ, and truth, be still the same, then a new and strange God, is a false God; a new and strange Christ, is a false Christ; a new and strange doctrine, is a false doctrine.

....

The true Christ is so glorious and excellent, that he cannot be seen but by that faith which is of divine operation. They that see the true Christ (and, O sirs, try your faith by this), they see one who is the same yesterday, today, and for ever. Oh! what delusive sights of Christ do many now see! They see a beautiful and glorious person presented to their imagination, or to their bodily eye. What a devil, instead of Christ, is this! But, true faith is the evidence of things not seen, and the substance of things hoped for. The faith that sees Christ truly, sees both what is past and present, and to come; a Christ yesterday, today, and for ever (Erskine 1865, 3:504, 513, 515-16).

On July 15, members of the Associate Presbytery met to consider the disastrous effect the current revival was having on their influence in the church. Formerly, hungry souls had been flocking to hear them. Now Whitefield and his Scottish associates were attracting far greater crowds. The result of their discussions was the publication of an *Act of the Associate Presbytery anent a Publick Fast*.... The *Act* denounces the revivalists and especially Whitefield for their rejection of the Solemn League and Covenant. It charges that "... bitter Outcryings, Faintings, severe bodily Pains, Convulsions, Voices, Visions, and Revelations, are the usual symptoms of a delusive spirit..." such as accompanies this work (Associate Presbytery 1742, 6). Finally, it calls for a public fast on Wednesday, August

4, to beseech God to "... revive a covenanted Work of Reformation, and direct this Presbytery in essaying to lift up a Testimony for the same..." (Associate Presbytery 1742, 7). Opposition to the revival, including reported visions of converts, was now official.

A copy of the *Act* was before James Robe when he penned the preface to his *Faithful Narrative* on July 29. He calls it "...the most heaven daring paper, that hath been published by any set of men in Britain these hundred years past" (Robe 1790, 55). He asks if any of the Associate Presbytery have taken the trouble to investigate the revival at first hand. Then he responds to the charge regarding visions. "As to voices, visions, and revelations none of our people, who are come to relief by faith in Christ, pretend to them; and all are cautioned against such deceits" (Robe 1790, 56). Alexander Webster, writing shortly thereafter, repeats essentially the same assertion in answer to the charges of the Secession ministers.

> Voices, Visions, Revelations are added, I suppose, for Argument's Sake.—None of the Subjects of this Work pretend to these Things. One or two Impostors, I'm informed, under such Pretences endeavoured to discredit this Work at the Beginning; but it is well known what Care was taken to detect them, and how effectually they were discouraged (Webster 1742a, 31).

A similar testimony comes from the anonymous author of *The Signs of the Times Considered*:

> There is one Objection against the present Work, that I have taken no Notice of, which, had it Facts to support it, would indeed prove all a Delusion: It is this; That the Faith of the new Converts is not founded on the Word, but visible Representations or imaginary Ideas of an amiable Object, which the Devil suggests to them is Christ.—But this is so far from being true, that, tho' I and others have been at a good deal of Pains, we could not find so much as one single Instance of this Kind; and tho' some few Instances had appeared, yet it could be no Evidence that

> there is no good Seed sown, because the Enemy is sowing Tares also (Signs 1742, iii-iv, original italicized).

The author does, however, admit that two persons, one at Kilsyth and the other at Logie or Saint Ninians, had experienced striking dreams. However, the Scriptures (Job 33:14 and Joel 2:28) suggest that convictions may be raised by dreams even though relief should not be expected in that manner (*Signs* 1742, 32).

A rejoinder was not long in coming. James Fisher quickly produced *A Review of the Preface to a Narrative of the Extraordinary Work at Kilsyth...* (1742), in which he responds to Robe and mentions Webster's pamphlet as well. He repeats the charge—to which Robe had already replied—that the work at Cambuslang was no different than the delusions of the French Prophets or Camizars (Fisher 1743, 37-43; Robe 1742, 52-55). (Significantly, the *Wonderful Narrative: Or, a Faithful Account of the French Prophets...* was published in Glasgow in 1742, the same year as its publication in Boston.) Fisher asserts that he and his companions had no need to go to Cambuslang, because they already had adequate proof that the work was not of God. He mentions "... *bodily Agonies* and extatick Impulses...", but clearly the chief prejudice lay elsewhere.

> When it was obvious that the *Promoters* of this Work in *Scotland*, were not only embracing and propagating *anarchial* and *Toleration* Principles, but practically owning them, by joining in full Communion with Mr. *Whitefield* a professed *Priest* of the Church of *England*...: In a Word, when it was perfectly evident, that the whole Work was managed and carried on, for bearing down any *Testimony* for *Scotland's Covenanted Reformation*; when all this was abundantly clear to the *Seceding Ministers*, would Mr. *Robe* have them to *come and see*, especially when joining in ministerial Communion, was a necessary *Preliminary* to any Satisfaction that might be expected (Fisher 1743, 59, body)?

Returning to Robe's disclaimer of visions, Fisher denies his assertion that none had occurred.

> There is too much of the *Deceit* here; for the Question is not whether they who *are come to Relief by Faith in Christ* pretend to such Things? but whether they who are the *Subjects of this Work*, who have undergone bodily Pains and Convulsions, do not likewise pretend to Visions, Voices and Revelations? It is most certain that many of them do, as can be proven by innumerable Witnesses, who have heard them own so much; and Mr. *Edwards* is so ingenious as to acknowledge that they appertain to the *Extraordinary Work*, and vindicates them as flowing from the Spirit of God tho' *indirectly*, *Dist. Marks*, Pag. 27, 28 (Fisher 1743, 62, body).

The reference to Edwards' *Distinguishing Marks* is not a mere aside. As a matter of fact, Fisher treats Edwards' sermon as one of the chief objects of his attack. He notes that the "… pamphlet is very highly extol'd by the *Promoters* of this Work; Mr. *Whitefield* says, he sent the first Copy of it to *Scotland*…" (Fisher 1743, 10, body). In response to Whitefield's suggestion a Scottish edition was printed in 1742 with a commendatory preface by John Willison. Robe commends the work in his *Faithful Narrative* as does Webster (Robe 1790, 46; Webster 1742a, 37). Since Whitefield has affirmed that Edwards "… answered all the Objections that any can make against [the revival]," Fisher feels justified in attempting to counter a number of Edwards' arguments (Fisher 1743, 10-11, body).

At this point it is only necessary to note the first and primary area of contention.

> I. The whole Scheme of Enthusiasm or Delusion, is built on this false Position, That we cannot think upon any Thing invisible or spiritual, without some Degree of Imagination, or, that Images of spiritual Things must be represented to our Fancy, else we can have no thought about them. Accordingly, Mr. Edwards tells us. Edin. Ed. Pag. 26. "Such is our Nature, that we cannot think of

> Things invisible, without a Degree of Imagination. I dare
> appeal (says he) to any Man of the greatest Powers of
> Mind, whether or no he is able to fix his Thoughts on God,
> or Christ, or the Things of another World, without
> imaginary Ideas attending his Meditation.—And the more
> engaged the Mind is, the more lively and strong, will the
> imaginary Idea ordinarly [sic] be." Than which nothing
> can be more false and absurd. . . (Fisher 1743, 11, body; cf.
> Edwards 1972, 236).

Fisher's conclusion is just the opposite of Edwards'.

> I say, the very *reverse* of this is true, for the more
> engaged the Mind is upon any spiritual Object—the more
> *divested* will it be, of all *imaginary Ideas*; Yea, there will
> be *no* imaginary Ideas cleaving to the Thought at all. . .
> (Fisher 1743, 13, body).

Behind this assertion are philosophical presuppositions and
theological consequences of great moment.

In defense of Edwards' doctrine Webster issued a second
edition of his *Divine Influence* with a preface in response to
Fisher's *Review*. In addition, Robe wrote a series of three
letters to Fisher. These were followed by a brief letter from
John Willison of Dundee to Fisher (Willison 1743, 19).
Therefore, when Fisher reissued his *Review* in 1743 he attached
a preface of his own "... illustrating the Enthusiastic Doctrine of
Imaginary Ideas" (Fisher 1743, title page). Lest there be any
suspicion that he has misrepresented the position of the
revivalists, he quotes further from the *Distinguishing Marks*
and from Edwards' earlier *Narrative* to demonstrate that
visionary experiences had occurred and were being defended.
In his preface, Fisher adds to the charge of poor philosophy the
weightier accusation that a mental image of Christ is
blasphemous idolatry (Fisher 1743, 10-13, preface).

1743 also saw the entry of another author into the pamphlet
warfare. In that year, Ralph Erskine published *Fraud and
Falshood Discovered*, with an appendix devoted to the heretical

doctrine of imaginary ideas. Both this appendix and Fisher's preface focus on Robe's second letter to James Fisher. *Fraud and Falshood* provoked two significant responses, *A Letter from Mr. Alexander Webster to the Rev. Ralph Erskine*, and *Mr. Robe's Fourth Letter to Mr. Fisher* (both in 1743). Finally, in 1745 after some delay in the press Erskine issued his definitive reply. Entitled *Faith No Fancy: Or, a Treatise of Mental Images...*, it was the lengthiest production on the subject during the controversy. The title page describes its purpose as showing "... That *an imaginary Idea of Christ as Man*, (when supposed to belong to saving Faith, whether in its Act or Object), imports nothing but Ignorance, Atheism, Idolatry, great Falshood, and gross Delusion."

"Imaginary Ideas" and "Mental Images." What did the various disputants mean by the terms? How are they related to saving faith? The answers to these questions bear not only on the controversies of the eighteenth century, but also on similar questions facing the church today. There are still those who see visions and dream of things divine. How should their claims be evaluated? The following chapters focus on the contributions of Jonathan Edwards and the Scottish theologians of his day.

CHAPTER 3
JONATHAN EDWARDS AND THE VISION OF GOD

To See or Not to See

Some minds are patchwork quilts, individual scraps of thought pieced together to form a serviceable and frequently attractive mosaic. Harmony among the diverse bits is imposed by the fashioner. It is not inherent. The philosophy and theology of Jonathan Edwards, however, are like the seamless robe of Christ, woven throughout with threads common to the whole. Take up his thought at any point, and the argument leads inevitably to other aspects of his understanding of God and the world. Examine opposite corners of the garment, and connecting strands can be discerned which link the two together. Because Edwards' thought is both consistent and comprehensive it is difficult to discuss one concept in isolation from the whole. At least some awareness of the entire range of subjects treated by him is needed in order to comprehend any given topic. That is true of his teaching regarding "imaginary ideas" of Christ.

Imaginary ideas must first be approached from the standpoint of psychology. John Locke revolutionized man's study of man, and Edwards adopted Locke's teaching on simple ideas. However, neither thinker felt it necessary to rework completely the traditional definition of the imagination, or the "fancy." Locke's doctrine that all knowledge comes through the senses lent a new significance to physical sight and opened up exciting possibilities for exploring the spiritual sight of believers. According to Edwards—and many others agreed—a man may have an imaginary idea of Christ in his mind, without possessing a saving sight of the Lord Jesus. He may see, and yet not see.

When God's grace reaches a soul, that soul catches a glimpse of the infinite beauty of the Savior. Such a view of Christ is the basis for genuinely gracious affections in the heart of the child of God. Edwards denies that the beauty of an imaginary idea of Christ is of the same nature as the beauty of Jesus Himself. However, for Edwards the world is a shadow or type of eternal ideas which exist in the mind of God, and his definition of beauty suggests that there may be a relationship between the secondary beauty of a mental image and that primary beauty which God alone possesses.

Lockean psychology, a new sense of things divine, the infinite beauty of Jesus Christ, and the idealism of Jonathan Edwards—these topics form the backdrop for the following discussion of imaginary ideas of Christ.

How a Man Sees

Perry Miller's Thesis

> In his second year at college, and thirteenth of his age, [Edwards] read Locke on the human understanding, with great delight and profit.... Taking that book into his hand, upon some occasion, not long before his death, he said to some of his select friends, who were then with him, that he was beyond expression entertained and pleased with it, when he read it in his youth at college; that he was as much engaged, and had more satisfaction and pleasure in studying it than the most greedy miser in gathering up handfuls of silver and gold from some new discovered treasure (Samuel Hopkins, quoted by Laurence 1980, 107).

In 1949 Perry Miller, taking his cue from this casual remark to "select friends," proclaimed to the scholarly world that Locke's influence on Edwards was both formative and crucial in his development as one of America's leading philosophers.

> The boy of fourteen grasped in a flash what was to take the free and catholic students of Professor Wigglesworth thirty or forty years to comprehend, that Locke was the

master-spirit of the age, and that the *Essay* made
everything then being offered at Harvard or Yale as
philosophy, psychology, and rhetoric so obsolete that it
could no longer be taken seriously (Miller [1949] 1973,
52-53).

Miller asserts that Edwards read and understood both John
Locke and Isaac Newton better than these men understood
themselves. From Locke, he learned that all knowledge comes
through the senses; from Newton he learned to replace the
notion of cause with the concept of God's sovereign will; and
from both he developed a species of idealism which did not
eliminate the reality of the external world (Miller [1949] 1973,
52-99).

Miller's reconstruction of Edwards' intellectual history has
not been without its critics. David Laurence suggests that "...
the striking image of the 'greedy miser' has possibly seduced
our imaginations into making a chance remark the basis for a
grand and satisfying biographical fiction" (Laurence 1980, 107).
Three general criticisms have been leveled at Miller's thesis.
First of all, he took too little account of Edwards' Puritan
training. The Scriptures and the standard divines played a large
part in the formation of Edwards' theology. Conrad Cherry
clearly demonstrates that Edwards' doctrine of justification was
based on a recovery of crucial insights from Calvin rather than
on his reading of Newton, as Miller suggests (Cherry [1966]
1974, 98-99). Second, Miller assumes that Edwards would
never have arrived at the essential features of his system
without Locke and Newton. But Edwards' discriminating use of
these two thinkers shows that he already had in place an
intellectual grid through which he sifted their writings. For
example, he "... explicitly rejected Locke's definition of identity
and Locke's position that 'uneasiness' determines the will"
(Cherry [1966] 1974, 15). Norman Fiering, after tracing the

multiplicity of influences on Edwards' thinking, concludes that he has "... been widely considered some sort of a descendant of John Locke, but Edwards's mind was profoundly antithetical to Locke's on most matters of importance" (Fiering 1980b, 47). Finally, Miller so stresses Edwards' originality that he isolates him from the rest of his culture. Was Edwards the only American of his day to be influenced by the new tides of philosophy? This last point deserves some further elaboration.

According to Norman B. Gibbs, "Locke is assumed to be the modern secular philosopher who influenced Edwards away from scholastic rationalism, whereas Locke himself was a part of the seventeenth century empiricist trend within the Christian tradition" (Gibbs 1953, 282). Empiricism was in the air, and many of the clergy were influenced by it in one way or another. "England, France, and Holland composed a remarkably well-integrated republic of letters, and New England shared many common borders with these countries in the realm of thought" (Fiering 1980b, 15). In addition, consider the judgment of R. A. Knox that "... the Evangelical is always an experimentalist. He feels certain that something has happened to him, and he invites you to let it happen to you. ..." (Knox 1950, 588). Knox carefully illustrates the validity of his assertion from the life of Wesley, but Edwards was no less an observer of religious conversion than the founder of Methodism.

Even Charles Chauncy criticized Edwards not so much on theoretical grounds as on the basis of the empirical data of the revival. Miller states that Edwards "... put the case for the revival in a language that Chauncy assumed they understood in common, but for which Chauncy did not have the key" (Miller [1949] 1973, 59). However, it is possible that Chauncy's brief expostulation against Edwards' philosophy (Chauncy [1743] 1975, 384) was based not so much on its Lockean roots as on Edwards' remarkable transformation of Locke. If Chauncy was

not conversant with Locke's *Essay* in 1743 (a questionable
assumption), he certainly was by the time he wrote *The
Benevolence of the Deity*, perhaps ten years later. Gibbs argues
that this was no radical departure from his earlier views.
Chauncy's theology changed. (He became a universalist.) His
psychology did not (Gibbs, 1953, 122-5, 137-9, et passim). In
the light of these and other, similar objections, Douglas
Elwood's moderate assessment of Edwards deserves careful
consideration.

> He used Locke and Newton, Cudworth and Smith,
> Mastricht and Turretin when he found in their writings
> support of his own views, but he was not dependent on
> any single author or group of authors in a hand-to-mouth
> fashion.... He welcomed Newton's physics and Locke's
> psychology, but there is no evidence that he was rejecting
> the Augustinian metaphysics which underlay original
> Puritanism (1960, 6).

Nevertheless, although Miller's thesis cannot be allowed to
stand without serious modification, it remains true that Locke
helped Edwards to a new way of seeing the world.

Edwards and Locke

Jonathan Edwards' Puritan forebears were burdened with
two conflicting conceptions of the nature of reason. From
Aristotle through the scholastics they had learned that reason is
a power or ability to discover truth through experience.
However, Platonism mediated through Augustine taught that
reason is the source of truth in the human mind. It is the giver
of ideas through intuition or recollection (Miller 1961, 190-194).
Although man was corrupted by the fall and had lost much of
his original understanding, he still retained a knowledge of
God's existence, a basic comprehension of the law of nature
written on the heart, and logic for investigating and
systematizing knowledge (Miller 1961, 181-190). One of the
chief proofs that God had given innate knowledge to men was

found in Adam's naming of the creatures. In the words of John Milton,

> I named them as they passed, and understood
> Their nature; with such knowledge God endued
> My sudden apprehension. But in these
> I found not what methought I wanted still.
> (Paradise Lost 8. 352-5)

Book One of Locke's *Essay concerning Human Understanding* (published in 1690) consists of a determined rejection of the concept of innate ideas. With a few notable inconsistencies, Locke attempted to establish all of knowledge upon an empirical basis. Book Two begins with his celebrated comparison of the human mind to a blank sheet of paper. How is the *tabula rasa* of the mind filled?

> To this I answer, in one word, From Experience: In that, all our knowledge is founded.... Our observation employ'd either about external, sensible Objects; or about the internal Operations of our Minds, perceived and reflected on by our selves, is that, which supplies our Understandings with all the materials of thinking (Locke 1975, p. 104).

The first source of ideas, depending on external objects is denoted "sensation," and the second, "... which might properly enough be call'd internal Sense...," is termed "reflection." In the first case, a man looks at the world; in the second, at his own mind (Locke, p. 105).

The age at which Edwards read and began reacting to Locke has been a matter of some dispute (the testimony of Samuel Hopkins notwithstanding). His famous notebook, "The Mind," has sometimes been taken to contain very early reflections on Locke. More recently it has been proposed that Edwards turned toward "idealistic phenomenalism" during the summer of 1723 while he was working on his M.A. thesis. "The Mind" was begun during the fall of that year; Number 45 was probably completed by the time he settled in Northampton in 1726, and he continued to add entries until shortly after his move to Stockbridge. Although there is some development in Edwards' private jottings, his basic viewpoint is consistent throughout "The Mind" and in that section of his "Miscellanies" which was completed after 1723 (Anderson in Edwards 1980, 29-30, 35-36, 53). Therefore, except for minor points, the dating of the various entries is not extremely important for this study.

Edwards quickly adopted Locke's insistence that the senses are the foundation of our knowledge of the world. "Things that we know by immediate sensation," he wrote, "we know intuitively, and they are properly self-evident truths" ("Mind," No. 19 in Edwards 1980, 346). The greenness of grass or the sweetness of honey impresses itself irresistibly on the senses. Therefore, Edwards concludes that:

> Our Senses, when sound and in ordinary circumstances, are not properly fallible in any thing; that is, we mean our experience by our senses.... And our senses are said to deceive us in some things, because our situation does not allow us to make trial, or our circumstances do not lead us to it, and so we are apt to judge by our experience.... Thus our Senses make us think that the Moon is among the clouds, because we cannot try it so quick, easily, and frequently, as we do the distance of things that are nearer ("Mind," No. 53 in Edwards 1980, 369).

However, Edwards experienced difficulty with Locke's teaching on reflection as a source of knowledge. In "The Mind" he lists as a significant topic for further investigation:

> 31. Sensation: Whether all ideas wherein the mind is merely passive and which are received immediately without any dependence on reflection, are not ideas of sensation, or external ideas; whether there be any difference between these. Whether it be possible for the Soul of man in this manner to be originally, and without dependence on reflection, capable of receiving any other ideas than those of sensation or something equivalent,

and so some external idea: and whether the ideas of the angels must not be of some such kind (Edwards 1980, 390).

According to Murray Murphey:

> Few doctrines of Locke involve more difficulties than his claim that we derive simple ideas from both sensation and reflection. The simple ideas of sensation are sensory qualities such as red, but there are no sensory qualities of this sort which characterize acts of the mind. So two courses lay open: either the ideas we have of acts of our own minds are not simple ideas, or else the concept of the simple idea must be expanded so as to include other-than-sensory qualities. The first course was taken by Berkeley...; the second was taken by Edwards.... Edwards sharply distinguished the acts of the mind from its passive ideas. How then can there be ideas of acts? Edwards found the answer to this problem in the fact that "all sorts of ideas of things are but the repetition of those very things over again—as well the ideas of colours, figures, solidity, tastes, and smells, as the ideas of thought and mental acts." According to this view, to have a true idea of red, the image of red must be present—otherwise, one is merely using the word and no definite sensible idea is present at all. So Edwards argues that to have a true idea of love, the act of love must be actually repeated (Flower and Murphey 1977, 1:159; cf. Edwards [1955] 1972, 115, 247).

This modification of Locke is extremely important for Edwards. A simple idea of any spiritual reality implies the possession of that reality. Thus, the Christian's idea of God and God's idea of Himself both involve far more than a purely intellectual apprehension. These concepts are discussed more fully below. However, the notion that our ideas come from outside ourselves through the senses or through something like them raises an important question. When a man believes he has seen the Lord Jesus Christ, can his claim be accepted as valid? Has God impressed that image on his mind through either his outer or his inner senses? Edwards' answer involves an understanding of the imagination which was in part traditional, and in part more innovative.

Imagination, or Internal Sight

For Jonathan Edwards and his contemporaries, the word "imagination" signified something quite different from what it does in the twentieth century. At that time "... the term 'imagination' was in crucial transition. The old scholastic meaning still persisted, in Edwards and in others, while at the same time the new romantic meaning was growing, with the latter having the present-day connotation of creativity" (Simonson 1975, 111). In Puritan and scholastic theology, the imagination is principally "That faculty of the mind by which are formed images or concepts of external objects not present to the senses..." (O.E.D. 1971, 1: 1377). "External objects produce images, or phantasms, of themselves in the five exterior senses—sight, hearing, taste, touch, and smell." After the phantasms have been examined by the "common sense" they pass to the imagination (also called "fancy" or "fantasy") which stores them for later recollection. However, the fancy may recombine images it contains to produce something new and different (Flower and Murphey 1977, 1:41-42).

The imagination is the freest of all the faculties, for its constructions need not correspond to the real world. Therein lies its danger, for it often deludes men by casting up deceptive illusions of happiness or horror. "Furthermore, it is dangerous because Satan, retaining his angelic incorporeality, can insert images into it without any agency of the senses, thus tempting the will with imaginations of such vices as could never have been conceived merely from experience" (Miller 1961, 257). All of these concepts were familiar to Jonathan Edwards and the men with whom he disputed the nature of saving grace. Although Edwards learned a better theory of perception from

Newton and a more holistic psychology from Locke, the basic concept and function of the imagination remained the same.

Within the scope of Puritan usage, "imagination" could have either a broad or a more specialized significance. According to the less technical connotation the imagination was the faculty which produced all sorts of notions not based on reality. In this sense, it was normally used pejoratively. Thus, Chauncy notes that "... *bodily Agitations, Convulsions, Tremblings, Swoonings,* and the like, have been common... among those who have been evidently under the Power of an *ungovern'd* Imagination" (Chauncy 1743, 5, body). Edwards also reminded himself in his "Directions for Judging of Persons' Experiences," to take care "That their discoveries and illuminations and experiences in general, are not superficial pangs, flashes, imaginations, freaks, but solid, substantial, deep, inwrought into the frame and temper of their minds, and discovered to have respect to practice" (Edwards 1865, 184). In an early essay, he noted that "Of all prejudices, no one so fights with natural philosophy, and prevails more against it, than those of imagination...." The reason is that "... opinions arising from imagination take us as soon as we are born, are beat into us by every act of sensation, and so grow up with us from our very births; and by that means grow into us so fast that it is almost impossible to root them out..." (Edwards 1980, 196).

In more specialized usage, an idea in the imagination referred to a mental image, a veritable picture formed in the mind. Milton is only uttering a commonplace of psychology when he places in Adam's mouth these words:

> Mine eyes, he closed, but left the cell
> Of fancy, my internal sight; by which,
> Abstract as in a trance, me thought I saw,
> Though sleeping, where I lay, and saw the Shape
> Still glorious before whom awake I stood;
> Who stooping, opened my left side, and took

From thence a rib, with cordial spirits warm,
And life-blood streaming fresh; wide was the wound,
But suddenly with flesh filled up and healed.
(Paradise Lost 8. 460-69)

This is the sense in which Edwards uses the term in the crucial passages dealing with visions of Christ. "The imagination," he tells us,

is that power of the mind, whereby it can have a conception, or idea of things of an external or outward nature (that is, of such sort of things as are the objects of the outward senses), when those things are not present, and be not perceived by the senses. It is called imagination from the word "image"; because thereby a person can have an image of some external thing in his mind, when that thing is not present in reality, nor anything like it. All such kind of things as we perceive by our five external senses, seeing, hearing, smelling, tasting and feeling are external things: and when a person has an idea, or image of any of these sorts of things in his mind, when they are not there, and when he don't really see, hear, smell, taste, nor feel them; that is to have an imagination of them, and these ideas are imaginary ideas; and when such kind of ideas are strongly impressed upon the mind, and the image of them in the mind is very lively, almost as if one saw them, or heard them, etc. that is called an impression on the imagination (Edwards 1959, 210-11).

It is important to keep this definition in mind, especially since some recent scholars have not adhered to it. There has been a tendency to discuss Edwards' concept of beauty in terms of a sanctified or regenerate imagination (Johnson 1981-82, 279-80, fn. 2-3). According to this view, although the natural imagination is not a reliable guide in spiritual matters, "Edwards thought of the religious imagination as the capacity to discover what already exists and, in the end, to apprehend the full beauty and glory of the Creator" (Simonson 1975, 116-17). Such a use of the word "imagination" appears to be a modernization of Edwards which does disservice to the task of understanding him on his own terms.

The researches of Francis Galton (1822-1911) have demonstrated that there exist

> ... enormous differences in imagery between one mind and another.... "I found that the great majority of the men of science to whom I first applied protested that mental imagery was unknown to them...." But there were also persons who reported images "quite as bright as an actual scene" and "all the objects well defined" (Blanshard 1948, 261-2).

The Puritans did not have to wait for modern science to demonstrate the existence of such images. They were quite familiar with the phenomenon. In fact, it appears that Edwards himself may have been one of those kinds of persons who frequently think in terms of mental images. (James Robe, however, interprets Edwards differently, *vide infra*.) In his list of subjects to be handled in a treatise on the mind he proposes the question, "How far imagination is unavoidable in all thinking, and why?" (Edwards 1980, 391). When he wrote *Distinguishing Marks* at the height of the revival controversy he asserted:

> Such is our nature that we can't think of things invisible, without a degree of imagination. I dare appeal to any man, of the greatest powers of mind, whether he is able to fix his thoughts on God or Christ, or the things of another world, without imaginary ideas attending his meditations? And the more engaged the mind is, and the more intense the contemplation and affection, still the more lively and strong will the imaginary idea ordinarily be; especially when the contemplation and affection of the mind is attended with anything of surprise....
>
> As God has given us such a faculty as the imagination, and so made us that we can't think of things spiritual and invisible, without some exercise of this faculty, so it appears to me, that such is our state and nature, that this faculty is really subservient and helpful to the other

faculties of the mind, when a proper use is made of it; though oftentimes, when the imagination is too strong, and the other faculties weak, it overbears 'em, and much disturbs them in their exercise (Edwards 1972, 236).

In stating that imaginary ideas almost inevitably intrude into a man's thoughts of the divine, Edwards is stepping perilously close to the brink of acceptable Puritan dogma. While a more complete discussion of this issue is included in the next chapter, a few preliminary remarks need to be made at this point.

> In distinction from the Thomists, the Puritans hold that pure intelligibles may be completely abstracted from sensible phantasms, so that no phantasms remain associated with the pure concept. God, angels, the soul itself, and all spiritual things are known as such pure intelligible objects wholly free of sense imagery. We do indeed obtain these conceptions by abstraction from phantasms, but not until we wholly free the intelligible from the sensible have we reached a true concept of a spirit.... A man who cannot conceive an angel without a phantasm of a winged creature has in Puritan eyes no concept of an angel at all (Flower and Murphey 1977, 1:42).

Visible representations of angels were not forbidden in Puritan circles. Hambrick-Stowe has collected a number of examples from devotional manuals and tracts of the period (Hambrick-Stowe 1982, 41, 56-57, 204, 233). Significantly, he refers to them as "emblematic" of spiritual truth (Hambrick-Stowe 1982, 203). In Puritan terminology, they would not properly be called "images." John Owen in his opposition to popish images of Christ refers to the figures of cherubim in the Old Testament:

> You next proceed to your plea from the *cherubims* set up by *Moses* in the holy place over the ark; and thence you will needs wrest an argument for your images, and the worship of them.... It is of images we are speaking precisely, and not of figures. Figures may include *types*

and *hieroglyphicks*, and any representation of things.
Images represent persons; and such alone are those about
which we treat. And, if a *person* be not presented by an
image, it is not his image.... Now, I pray, tell me, What
personal subsistences these cherubims with their various
wings and faces did represent? Do you believe, that they
gave you the shape and likeness of angels? It is true, that
John the Bishop of *Thessalonica*, in your synod of *Nice*,
with the approval of the rest of his company, affirms, that
it was the opinion of the Catholick church, that angels and
archangels were not altogether *incorporeal and invisible,
but to have a slender body of air or fire*, Act. v. But are
you of the same mind? Or do you not rather think, that
the Catholick church was belied and abused by the synod?
And, if they are absolutely incorporeal and invisible, how
can an image be made of them? Should a man look on the
cherubims as images of angels? Would not the first thing
they teach, be a lie? namely, that angels are like unto
them; which is the first language of any image whatever.
The truth is, the *Mosaical* cherubims were mere
hieroglyphicks, to represent the constant tender love and
watchfulness of God over the ark of his covenant, and had
nothing of the nature of images in them" (cited by Erskine
1745, 332).

Although figures of angels might be tolerated, Puritan
opposition to images of God is clear and unambiguous. The
second commandment is regularly understood as forbidding
images of any member of the Trinity, an interpretation which
Edwards follows. He writes:

This commandment forbids our making use of other
images in our worshipping God besides Christ, who is
"the image of the invisible God, the brightness of His
glory, and the express image of His person," by which
image alone God makes known Himself, and shews His
glory as the fit object of our worship; for we behold "the
glory of God *in the face of Jesus Christ.*" The Heathen had
images that they might have something present with them
as representatives of the Deity that was absent; but Christ
only is our Immanuel or "God with us" (Grosart 1865, 85).

In addition, the Westminster Larger Catechism, Question 109, specifically warns against the dangers of mental idolatry. On this basis ministers of the Secession Church in Scotland charge the revival party with encouraging idolatry. The mental images of Christ, experienced by some of the converts, seem to be a clear violation of the second commandment. Edwards, however, appears unmoved by such considerations. Why?

Preliminary Answers

The preceding discussion of how a man sees, both with his external senses and with the fancy, suggests several reasons for Edwards' willingness to treat imaginary ideas of Christ seriously. First, the psychology which he adapted from Locke does not lend itself well to a separation of the mind into airtight compartments. As Norman Fiering has pointed out, Locke's critique of faculty psychology was aimed at the abuses of the system, and his insights into the unified working of the understanding and the will are found as early as St. Thomas Aquinas (Fiering 1981a, 106-08). Similar examples can be cited from Puritan sources. However, the significant point is that Locke's description of the process of knowing left no room for distinguishing some faculties as animal and others as rational. In Puritan psychology the faculties of reason, will and conscience belong to the immortal soul, while others including the imagination "... are faculties of the sensitive soul and so are common to man and beast" (Flower and Murphey 1977, 1:71). As shall be seen in the next chapter, this distinction is crucial in Ralph Erskine's rejection of mental images of Christ. Locke's stress on the unitary nature of the mind and its functions broke down these kinds of artificial distinctions and helped to destroy the theoretical foundation for dissociating the imagination from the understanding.

Second, the empirical epistemology of Locke demands that the mind be open to receive impressions from outside, itself. Such impressions need to be evaluated, of course, but they cannot be denied. Edwards is by no means uncritical in his acceptance of the imaginary ideas of the converts. However, he cannot entirely thrust them aside when he believes on other, equally empirical grounds, that the subjects of such visions are sometimes genuinely gracious.

A third reason for Edwards' acceptance of mental imagery as a valid (though not saving) religious experience may be seen in his theory of language. Edwards and Locke both hold that words are arbitrary signs of ideas (Locke 1975, 405). Edwards carefully demonstrates that the "Great part of our thoughts and the discourse of our minds concerning [things] is without the actual ideas of those things of which we discourse and reason; but the mind makes use of signs instead of the ideas themselves" (Edwards [1955] 1972, 114). The reason that men use signs in place of ideas in their thinking is that they cannot hold many ideas in their minds at one time. (Remember that for Edwards an idea is characterized by the vividness, clearness, and distinctness of immediate sense impressions.) Consider his analysis of the various simple ideas included in the complex idea of "people":

> ... an actual idea of those things wherein manhood most essentially consists, as an idea of reason, which contains many other actual ideas—as an actual idea of consciousness, an actual idea of disposal of ideas in the mind, an actual idea of a consequent perception of relations and connections between them, etc. And so he must have an actual idea of will, which contains an actual idea of pleasure and pain, agreeableness and disagreeableness, and a consequent command or imperate act of the soul, etc. (Edwards [1955] 1972, 113).

No wonder Edwards found it difficult to think without signs!

Significantly, mental images can serve as signs for ideas just as words do. Edwards specifically says that "... a confused idea of an outer appearance like that of man..." is not the idea of man; it is "... only a sign made use of instead of an idea" (Edwards [1955] 1972, 114). Therefore, someone who has an imaginary idea of Christ in his mind is essentially no different than the person who uses the word "Jesus" to represent the Person of the Savior. As a matter of fact, a mental image, because of its vividness, may be even more in keeping with the heightened sense of God's holiness and beauty which marks a genuinely gracious experience. Edwards never identifies imaginary ideas with a saving sight of Christ, but he is also unwilling to divorce the two completely and absolutely. In a sermon on II Corinthians 13:5 he declares:

> Thus persons are deceived by the use of figurative and metaphorical expressions. When we speak of light let into the soul in this case, nothing is meant of any resemblance to any brightness that we see with our bodily eyes, of the nature of brightness of the sun or any other shining object; this is a very gross notion of spiritual light, such light is not spiritual but outward, Spiritual light is the light of the mind. The light of the mind is knowledge, truth and evidence. It is a sight, sense, and a right understanding of things that is spiritual light. When a person is made to understand spiritual things in a new manner, and is convinced of the truth of them, and has a realizing apprehension of them, and lively sense of their excellency, then he has new light. That conviction of the judgment, and that sense of heart are called light only figuratively, not that there is any proper visible shining or anything that looks like the shining of some distant object. Not but that persons when under the lively sense of the glory of spiritual objects may naturally continue in their minds a lively idea of an outward glory and brightness. But that is only an idea in the imagination, and is not the thing that the essence of spiritual light consists in (Edwards 1948, 31-32).

To that true spiritual light and sight it is necessary now to turn.

What the Christian Sees

Antecedents to Edwards' "New Sense"

When Jonathan Edwards made a new sense of divine things the principal mark of a regenerate soul, he was not inventing terminology that was unfamiliar to his readers. Rather, he was building on, and giving new direction to, a well-established Puritan concept (Elwood 1960, 121; Fiering 1981b, 124-25). "o taste and see that the LORD is good. . ." (Psalm 34:8) was a common injunction. Puritan evaluation of the new sense was not uniform, however.

Thomas Hooker and Richard Sibbes stressed that a taste of the love of God and a relish for spiritual things are preparatory to salvation. A preliminary experience of the goodness of God formed the basis for drawing the sinner to rest in Christ (Pettit 1966, 72, 98-99). The whole subject of preparation is quite large, and it is not necessary to enter into the contemporary debate over whether the sinner should attempt to prepare himself for grace. It is enough to affirm that "All Reformed theology always maintained that God himself prepares the elect unregenerate for regeneration through his providential provision of the means of grace" (Gerstner and Gerstner 1979, 6). A failure to recognize this point has led Perry Miller and Norman Pettit somewhat astray (Hambrick-Stowe 1982, 80).

At this point in the discussion it is necessary only to ask whether God uses a new taste for His excellencies in order to lead men to saving faith in Christ. The evidence suggests that Edwards did not follow this line of thought. In his *Narrative*, he carefully describes the process of conversion as he observed it during the revival in Northampton. Most of the preliminary stages before the arrival of genuine grace relate to the misery of sinners under a sense of the just wrath of God. It is true that their despair may be temporarily alleviated. Edwards writes:

> But then perhaps by something they read or hear of the infinite mercy of God and all-sufficiency of Christ for the chief of sinners, they have some encouragement and hope renewed; but think that as yet they are not fit to come to Christ; they are so wicked that Christ will never accept of them: and then it may be they set themselves upon a new course of fruitless endeavors in their own strength to make themselves better, and still meet with new disappointments (Edwards 1972, 165).

He states that he found

> ... himself under a necessity greatly to insist upon it with them, that God is under no manner of obligation to shew mercy to any natural man, whose heart is not turned to God: and that a man can challenge nothing, either in absolute justice or by free promise, from anything he does before he has believed on Jesus Christ or has true repentance begun in him. It appears to me, that if I had taught those that came to me under trouble any other doctrine, I should have taken a most direct course utterly to have undone them.... And yet those that have been under awakenings have oftentimes plainly stood in need of being encouraged, by being told of the infinite and all-sufficient mercy of God in Christ; and that 'tis God's manner to succeed diligence and to bless his own means, that so awakenings and encouragements, fear and hope may be duly mixed and proportioned to preserve their minds in a just medium between the two extremes of self-flattery and despondence... (Edwards 1972, 167-68).

It seems unfitting to describe these preliminary glimpses of God's grace as a foretaste of the relish which the saints have for God. God's grace is not tasted; it is only viewed from the outside. The first experience of "... a sort of complacency of soul..." (and that, in respect to God's justice!) is viewed as resulting "... from an high exercise of grace, in saving repentance and evangelical humiliation. . ." (Edwards 1972, 170). This conclusion is reinforced by Edwards' insistence "That those that have not a saving interest in Christ have no degree of that relish and sense of spiritual things or things of the Spirit, of their Divine truth and excellency, which a true saint has. . ." (Edwards 1865, 22, original italicized). Again, "They not only have not these communications of the Spirit of God in so high a degree as the saints, but have nothing of that nature or kind" (Edwards 1959, 203).

Thomas Goodwin seems closer than Hooker and Sibbes to the position adopted by Edwards when he writes:

> If you ask one what it is the saints know, which another man knows not, I answer you fully he himself cannot tell you. For it is certain as to that impression which the Holy Ghost leaves upon the heart of a man, that can never make the like impression on another; he may describe it to you, but he cannot convey the same image and impression upon the heart of any man else (Pettit 1966, 10-11).

John Owen also asserts that the saints receive a "... *spiritual sense* of the *power and reality of the things believed...*" which is incommunicable to anyone else. He continues,

> And on the account of this spiritual experience is our perception of spiritual things so often expressed by acts of sense, as tasting, seeing, feeling, and the like .... And when believers have attained thereunto,... they need neither argument, nor motive, nor anything else, to persuade them or confirm them in believing. And whereas this spiritual experience, which believers obtain through the Holy Ghost, is such as cannot rationally be contended about, seeing those who have received it cannot fully express it, and those who have not cannot understand it, nor the efficacy which it hath to secure and establish the mind, it is left to be determined on them alone who have their "senses exercised to discern good and evil" (Owen [1850-53] 1967, 4:64).

John Locke, who may have come under the influence of Owen at Oxford (Logan 1980, 90), was certainly familiar with the concept of incommunicable spiritual experiences. In view of

Locke's thorough attempt at an empirical foundation for all knowledge, it seems surprising that he makes room for any revelation at all. When he does, it is carefully circumscribed to guard against enthusiasm. Although revealed truths can be known with certainty because God's testimony is reliable, yet reason must judge which of the claimants to revelation are genuine. Revealed truth may be beyond the scope of reason (such as the resurrection of the body), but nothing that is contrary to reason may be accepted as revelation (Copleston 1964, 120-22). Locke distinguishes between "original revelation" and "traditional revelation":

> By the one, I mean that first Impression, which is made immediately by GOD, on the Mind of any Man, to which we cannot set any Bounds; and by the other, those Impressions delivered over to others in Words, and the ordinary ways of conveying our Conceptions to another (Locke 1975, 690).

Regarding the communication of "original revelation" Locke makes several striking observations, which are significant because they are paralleled in Edwards' discussion of a Christian's new sense of divine things. He says, "... That *no Man inspired by God, can by any Revelation communicate to others any new simple Ideas* which they had not before from Sensation or Reflexion" (Locke 1975, 698). The reason is that human language can only bring to mind ideas or combinations of ideas which have already been impressed on the mind by sensation or reflection. The Apostle Paul is used as an example, for he was unable to relate the things disclosed to him when he was caught up into the third heaven.

> And, supposing GOD should discover to any one, super-naturally, a Species of Creatures inhabiting, For Example *Jupiter*, or *Saturn*... which had six Senses; and imprint on his Mind the *Ideas*, convey'd to theirs by the sixth Sense, he could no more, by Words, produce in the Minds of other Men those *Ideas*, imprinted by that sixth Sense,

than one of us could convey the *Idea* of any Colour, by the sound of Words into a Man, who having the other four Senses perfect, had always totally wanted the fifth of Seeing (Locke 1975, 690).

Thus, much of the content of "original revelation" may not be able to be conveyed by "traditional revelation." For all practical purposes Locke limited even "original revelation" to the authors of Scripture. He did not deny that God is

> "... able to enlighten the understanding by a ray darted into the mind immediately from the fountain of light...." He simply found the belief that a person needed such a ray of supernatural light to make him a Christian, both arrogant and irrational (Laurence 1980, 110).

He was horrified by the suggestion that a supernaturally imparted spiritual sense could ever be the normal experience of the ordinary Christian.

The contribution of Jonathan Edwards to the doctrine of the "new sense" was to combine insights gained both from Locke and from such Puritans as John Owen. Locke had equated original revelation with a new sense of supernaturally given ideas. Edwards eliminated the content from God's communications to the saints—that came from Scripture (Edwards 1959, 278, 280, 285-86; Laurence 1980, 113-22)—and broadened Locke's categories to encompass all believers. The result was a new sense belonging to all the redeemed and defined as a "new simple idea" of spiritual things.

> From hence it follows, that in those gracious exercises and affections which are wrought in the minds of the saints, through the saving influences of the Spirit of God, there is a new inward *perception* or *sensation* of their minds, entirely different in its nature and kind, from anything that ever their minds were the subjects of before they were sanctified.... [T]here is, what some metaphysicians call a new *simple idea*. ... and here is, as it were, a new *spiritual sense* that the mind has, or a principle of a new kind of perception or spiritual

> sensation, which is in its whole nature different from any former kinds of sensation of the mind, as tasting is diverse from any of the other senses.... So that the spiritual perceptions which a sanctified and spiritual person has, are not only diverse from all that natural men have, after the manner that ideas or perceptions of the same sense may differ one from another, but rather as the ideas and sensations of different senses do differ (Edwards 1959, 205-06).

As Elwood succinctly puts it,

> The "new simple idea" is *new* in the sense that it is not derived from any past activities of the mind; *simple* in that it is not a synthesis of ordinary physical sensations; *idea* in the sense of an immediate consciousness, or intuition, of the reality and beauty of God and of godliness, accompanied by a profound emotion embracing the intuited object (Elwood 1960, 136-37).

Edwards' synthesis of Lockean terminology and Puritan insights into the nature of regeneration forms the background for discussion in the next sections of the present paper.

The Nature of Edwards' "New Sense"

What is this "new sense" possessed by the Christian? Is it a new faculty added to those already present in the natural man? Is it some kind of change in the structure of a man's mannishness? Scholars are agreed that Edwards' answer is negative (e.g. Cherry [1966] 1974,20,31). This is a logical consequence of his unitary psychology. If the faculties are divided between the "immortal soul" and the "sensitive soul" as in the Puritan scheme (Flower and Murphey 82 1977, 1:71), it is not difficult to conceive of adding a new faculty to the regenerate soul. If, however, the faculties are simply different aspects of an unbreakable whole, the addition of a faculty distinct from the rest would be altogether disruptive. The significance of Edwards' approach to the question may be seen by contrast with the views of John Owen and Charles Chauncy.

Owen's understanding of the new sense is governed by his concepts of man's nature, depravity and regeneration. Owen is not entirely consistent in his description of the human soul. On occasion, he unites the faculties of the soul in much the same way as Locke and Edwards were to do. For instance, "And the heart in the Scripture is taken for the whole rational soul, not absolutely, but as all the faculties of the soul are one common principle of all our moral operations" (Owen [1850-53] 1965-67, 3:326, cf. also 3:250). Inconsistency appears, however, because he does not see that a unitary psychology should involve equal depravity in all of the faculties. Thus, he asserts "That the will and affections [are] more corrupted than the understanding" (3:268). The lack of a clearly defined, consistently maintained terminology allows him to teach that "... when God is pleased to give us a new ability to understand and perceive spiritual things in a due manner, he is said to give us a new faculty, because of the utter disability of our minds naturally to receive them..." (3:252).

Owen teaches that human depravity is so thorough that

> ... there is a two fold impotency in the minds of men with respect unto spiritual things:—(1.) That which immediately affects the mind, a *natural impotency* whence it *cannot* receive them for want of light in itself. (2.) That which affects the mind by the will and affections, a *moral impotency*, whereby it cannot receive the things of the Spirit of God, because unalterably it *will not*... (Owen [1850-53] 1965-67, 3:266).

Both kinds of impotency involve real and culpable sin (3:266-67). Therefore, both need to be dealt with in regeneration. Moral impotence is cured by the Holy Spirit using the Word of God as it is presented externally to the sinner. However, this is not enough. "There is not only a moral but a physical immediate operation of the Spirit, by his power and grace, or his powerful grace, upon the minds or souls of men in their regeneration" (3:316). Of course, "physical" in this connection does not mean "material." It pertains to the basic nature (Greek, phusis) of the soul. Both Chauncy and Edwards read Owen, and his ideas must be kept in mind as a background for understanding theirs.

Charles Chauncy denied most of the things which Owen asserted. In "The Method of the Spirit, in the Work of Illumination" he examines the Christian's new sense of spiritual things. He deduces conclusions about spiritual sight from comparisons with physical sight. God, he says, does not need to create a new faculty in order to bring him spiritual illumination (Chauncy 1765, 279-281). The reason is that man's inability is moral only.

> What I aim at, in this additional tho't, is to show, that, in the work of illumination, there is no "physically new sense" implanted in the sinner, any more than a physically new intellectual faculty.... But the bible no where gives us reason to expect the implantation of any such new capacity: Nor indeed is there any need of it. The moral change that is made in the understanding, by the illuminations of the Spirit of God, will, at the same time, introduce a proportionable taste, relish, or savour of divine and spiritual objects. This taste may be, and actually is, wanting in vitiated and corrupted minds.... But if the understanding is enlightened in the things of the Spirit, a taste for them will be a natural concomitant. When the mind is illuminated, so as to perceive revealed objects in their true point of light, it will perceive also a beauty and glory in them. These perceptions are, as I imagine, inseparable from each other. The constitution of man is such that he can't see the truth as it is in Jesus, and not perceive, at the same time, the excelling glory and importance of it (Chauncy 1765, 286-87).

The Holy Spirit "... assists, superintends and conducts the exercise. . ." of a man's thoughts (Chauncy 1765, 296). His work is not the creation of a new sense, but may rather be compared to glasses which strengthen weakened physical sight (Chauncy 1765, 297-99). Although this strong polemic against a "physical" change during regeneration is rather late, it does not represent any departure from his earlier views. In *The New Creature* he declared, "Indeed physically speaking, no alteration is effected, either in the powers of his soul or body: But in the *moral* and *religious* sense, a change is wrought in him. . ." (1741, 6-7). Superficially, there seems to be a great deal of similarity between Edwards and Chauncy. Edwards also denies that the new sense is a physically new faculty.

> This new spiritual sense, and the new dispositions that attend it, are no new faculties, but are new principles of nature. I use the word "principles," for want of a word of a more determinate signification. By a principle of nature in this place, I mean that foundation which is laid in nature, either old or new, for any particular manner or kind of exercise of the faculties of the soul; or a natural habit or foundation for action, giving a person ability and disposition to exert the faculties of such a certain kind; so that to exert the faculties in that kind of exercises, may be said to be his nature. So this new spiritual sense is not a new faculty of understanding, but it is a new foundation laid in the nature of the soul, for a new kind of exercises of the same faculty of understanding. So that new holy disposition of heart that attends this new sense, is not a new faculty of will, but a foundation laid in the nature of the soul, for a new kind of exercises of the same faculty of will (Edwards 1959, 206).

The crucial difference between Chauncy and Edwards in their discussion of the new sense is found in Edwards' definition of it as a habit or disposition of the heart. As Sang Hyun Lee has pointed out (1976), Edwards uses these terms to describe the structure or capacity of the mind which enables it to utilize the ideas it receives through sensation. Therefore, although he does not describe regeneration as the creation of a new faculty, he does infer that there is a restructuring of a

person's underlying nature when he is converted. By describing
the change in the regenerate man as a change in habit or
disposition, Edwards is able to avoid two extremes. There is,
indeed, no physical change in the faculties. Habit and
disposition are relational terms rather than references to a
distinguishable part of the soul. On the other hand, the moral
renovation of the sinner cannot be ascribed solely to the use of
the Word mediated by the Holy Spirit (as with Chauncy). There
is also an immediate action of the Holy Spirit in the soul.

> But the exciting a sense of things pertaining to our eternal
> interest is a thing that we are so far from and so unable to
> obtain of ourselves (by reason of the direction of the
> inclinations and natural dispositions of the soul [away]
> from those things as they are, and the sinking of our
> intellectual powers, and the great subjection of the soul in
> its fallen state to the external senses), that a due sense of
> those things is never attained without immediate divine
> assistance (Edwards [1955] 1972, 122).

Natural men may come to an "ideal apprehension" of the
natural perfections of God, for example, His greatness. In such
cases the Spirit assists their natural powers. However, when the
Spirit of God gives a genuine taste of the sweetness of the moral
perfections of God, He does it "... not by assisting natural
principles but by infusing something super natural" (Edwards
[1955] 1972, 124). In this way, Edwards is able to maintain his
famous distinction between moral and natural inability (in
Freedom of the Will) without adopting Chauncy's more
rationalistic approach to conversion. The removal of moral
inability according to Chauncy did not require anything more
than the influence of the Spirit, in Edwards' scheme, moral
inability must be cured by an infusion of the Spirit.

Two major consequences flow from Edwards' definition of
the new sense. First of all, the fact that no new faculty is created
underscores a conclusion suggested earlier. The visions

experienced by some subjects of the revival cannot be used to deny the reality of their conversion. Since the soul's faculties remain unchanged, the regenerate man may have natural experiences (visions) accompanying his spiritual ones (the new sense). His conversion has not altered the basic composition of his human nature. Second, the immediate work of the Holy Spirit in imparting the new sense means that conversion is distinctly a work of God. Just what that work is shall be explored next.

The Content of Edwards' "New Sense"

The "new simple idea" of the Christian is described by Edwards as a new sense, particularly as a new sight or taste of spiritual things. But what is it that he sees? Not the natural perfection of God, which constitutes His greatness, for that may be revealed to the unconverted man. The Christian is a person who has been granted a perception of the moral perfection of God which is summed up in holiness. Holiness is the beauty or excellency of God, and the essence of true spiritual knowledge is to rejoice in that beauty. People do not first enjoy the benefits conferred by Christ and then love God in return. Rather, the soul first sees the Lord in all His glory, and falling in love with such overwhelming beauty, he then receives assurance that he has been accepted by God (Edwards 1959, 245-46, 254-56). As Edwards explains:

> From what has been said, it may easily be understood what I intend, when I say that a love to divine things for the beauty of their moral excellency, is the beginning and spring of all holy affection.
>
> ... Holy persons, in the exercise of holy affections, do love divine things primarily for their holiness; they love God, in the first place, for the beauty of his holiness.... The holiness of an intelligent creature, is the beauty of all his natural perfections. And so it is in God... holiness is in a peculiar manner the beauty of the divine nature. Hence

we often read of the beauty of holiness... This renders all his other attributes glorious and lovely.

> ... A true love to God must begin with a delight in his holiness, not with a delight in any other attribute; for no other attribute is truly lovely without this... (Edwards 1959, 256-57).

At this point it must be recalled that according to Edwards,

> ... there is no actual idea of those things but what consists in the actual existence of the same things, or like things, in our own minds. For instance, to excite the idea of an idea we must have that very idea in our minds; we must have the same idea.... To have an actual idea of any pleasure or delight, there must be excited a degree of that delight; so to have an actual idea of any trouble or kind of pain, there must be excited a degree of that pain or trouble; and to have an idea of any affection of the mind, there must be then present a degree of that affection (Edwards [1955] 1972, 115).

It may now be asked how God's holiness can be so impressed on the soul of a man that he has a clear and distinct idea of it. Edwards' answer involves a striking explanation of original sin and of regeneration.

A Christian's idea of God's holiness is based on an actual partaking of that holiness in the person of the Holy Spirit. When Adam was created, he was endowed with two kinds of principles, natural and spiritual.

> By natural principles, I mean the principles of human nature, as human nature is in this world—that is, in its animal state, or that belonging to the nature of man as man.... Such is a man's love to his own honour, love of his own pleasure, the natural appetites that he has by means of the body, &c. His spiritual principles were his love to God, and his relish of Divine beauties and enjoyments, &c. These may be called supernatural because they are no part of human nature. They do not belong to the nature of man as man, nor do they naturally and necessarily flow from the faculties and properties of that nature. Man can be man without them; they did not flow from anything in

the human nature, but from the Spirit of God dwelling in
man, and exerting itself by man's faculties as a principle
of action (Edwards 1865, 163).

Before the fall, the Holy Spirit indwelling Adam subordinated
his natural principles to the spiritual.

> But when man fell, then the Spirit of God left him, and so
> all his spiritual nature or spiritual principles; and then
> only the flesh was left, or merely the principle of human
> nature in its animal state... Corrupt nature is nothing else
> but the principle of human nature in its animal state, or
> the flesh (as it is called in Scripture) left to itself, or not
> subordinated to spiritual principles; and so far as it is
> unsubordinate, so far is it corrupt (Edwards 1865, 164).

In regeneration, some degree of the Holy Spirit is restored to
the soul, but not enough entirely to subdue the flesh. That is the
reason for the warfare between the flesh and the Spirit in the
Christian (Edwards 1865,164).

Edwards does not adopt the terminology of many modern
evangelicals who teach that the Christian possesses both an
"old" and a "new" nature. The implication is that both of these
natures are human, but that one is pure and the other corrupt.
The problem with this formulation from Edwards' point of view
is that the will does not stand outside our basic desires
choosing among them. It does not choose between the "old"
nature and the "new" nature. Nor can the Christian have two
wills corresponding to his two natures. The new hunger for
holiness in the regenerate soul must be identified with the Holy
Spirit who indwells the Christian.

> So that true saving grace is no other than that very love of
> God—that is, God, in One of the Persons of the Trinity,
> uniting Himself to the soul of a creature, as a vital
> principle, dwelling there and exerting Himself by the
> faculties of the soul of man, in His own proper nature,
> after the manner of a principle of nature (Edwards 1865,
> 53).

Since all the godliness of a believer is the direct result of the Spirit's working (rather than the independent exercise of a "new" human nature),

> The giving one gracious discovery or act of grace, or a thousand, has no proper natural tendency to cause an abiding habit of grace for the future; nor any otherwise than by Divine constitution and covenant. But all succeeding acts of grace must be as immediately, and, to all intents and purposes, as much from the immediate acting of the Spirit of God on the soul, as the first; and if God should take away His Spirit out of the soul, all habits and acts of grace would of themselves cease as immediately as light ceases in a room when a candle is carried out. And no man has a habit of grace dwelling in him any otherwise than as he has the Holy Spirit dwelling in him in his temple, and acting in union with his natural faculties, after the manner of a vital principle (Edwards 1865, 55).

In summary, then, what the Christian sees is the beauty of God's holiness. He is able to have a true idea of this, not because he has been given a new faculty, but because the Holy Spirit indwells him. He tastes the sweetness of God's moral excellency by actual participation in it through the immediate communication of the Spirit of God. The new sense of the Christian is thus totally foreign to anything which is possible to the natural man. However, since the natural faculties of the soul remain unchanged (they are a part of man's mannishness), even a regenerate man may experience very vivid exercises of his imagination. He may see visions which are not true glimpses of the spiritual world, but only products of his human nature. If this is so, do imaginary ideas of Christ bear any relationship at all to the spiritual beauty of the Savior, or are they purely accidental concomitants of an emotion-charged experience? While absolute proof may not be possible, it can nevertheless be suggested that Edwards' philosophy makes room for some kind of connection between imaginary and spiritual visions of God. The precise nature of that relationship depends on his conception of the relation between the natural and spiritual worlds in general.

Seeing God in the World

Edwards' Idealism and the Trinity

Edwards extended Locke's assertion that colors exist only in the mind to the more radical conclusion that even solidity has only a mental existence. His summary of the nature of existence can be stated in a single sentence: "The world is therefore an ideal one..." ("Mind," No. 27 in Edwards 1980, 351). Central to his development of idealism was "... his conviction that consciousness, involving perception and knowledge, is necessary for the existence of anything whatever" (Anderson in Edwards 1980, 29). However, the continuity of existence does not depend on continued observance of the world by created beings, for God maintains the "... course and succession of existences..." by continually "supposing" them to be ("Mind," No. 40 in Edwards 1980, 356-57). In his earliest reflections on the subject, Edwards limited the ideal existence of the world to material things. Spirits, he thought, did not depend for their existence on the conception of other minds. However, he soon extended his idealism to encompass created spirits as well (Theodore Hornberger in Opie 1969, 51). In Miscellany 880 he wrote: "God is the sum of all being, and there is no being without his being. All things are in Him, and He in all" (Gerstner 1980, 6).

Such statements have frequently provoked the charge (or suspicion) that Edwards espoused pantheism. More recently Elwood has put forward the modified suggestion that Edwards was close to the modern panentheism of Whitehead and Hartshorne (Elwood 1960, 12-32). This is not the place to enter into a detailed discussion of what is a very complex issue. It is mentioned only to indicate the pervasiveness of idealism in the thinking of Edwards. Even so staunch an admirer of Edwards as John Gerstner feels he must leave the problem unresolved (Gerstner 1980, 10). However, he helpfully points out that Edwards' "... whole theology is particularistic to the core. Men are not ultimately swallowed up in some divine All" (Gerstner 1980, 7). Edwards' teaching on hell is entirely contrary to the pantheistic or panentheistic conception of the world.

In addition to the material world and created spirits, Edwards carried his idealism into his formulation of the doctrine of the Trinity. The early Miscellany 94 contains his most complete statement of his doctrine, but he reverted to the subject frequently throughout his life. Murphey summarizes the fundamental concept well:

> Since God knows all there is, it of course follows that God knows Himself. Moreover, God's knowledge is perfect and amounts to an absolute immediate intuition of all there is. Now a perfect idea in the mind of God is, according to Edwards's idealism, the thing itself; of whatever God has an idea, that idea is the substance of the thing. Therefore, if God perfectly knows Himself, that idea which He has of Himself is the substantial image of God, and is one with the essence of God (Flower and Murphey 1977, 1:156).

The perfect idea which God has of Himself, this true image of God, is God the Son.

Not only does God know Himself, He also loves Himself. "The Holy Spirit is the act of God between the Father and the Son, infinitely loving and delighting in each other...; but the delight of God is properly a substance, yea, an infinitely perfect substance, even the essence" (Edwards [1955] 1972, 254).

> Hence 'tis to be accounted for, that though we often read in Scripture of the Father loving the Son, and the Son loving the Father, yet we never once read either of the Father or the Son loving the Holy Spirit, and the Spirit

loving either of Them. It is because the Holy Spirit is the
Divine love itself, the love of the Father and the Son
(Edwards 1865, 47).

The Holy Spirit is more than the love of God; He is also the
holiness and happiness of God since "Both the holiness and
happiness of the Godhead consists in this love" (Edwards 1865,
47-48).

Although Edwards' formulation of the doctrine of the
Trinity is unusual, it is not heretical, and it is not entirely
unique. A similar conception may be found in Augustine's
famous work De Trinitate (Gerstner 1980, 57-58; Kelly 1978,
276-78). Edwards' description of the Trinity and his
understanding of God's relation to the world play a significant
part in his concept of how God reveals Himself to men.

Typology: The Sensible and the Spiritual World

As a good son of the Puritans, Edwards looked to Scripture
for final authority in discerning spiritual truth. However, like
them he also believed that God spoke through the sensible
world. The Puritans, following Peter Ramus, taught that
creation is a form of God's speech. The world is full of God's
artistry, and the techniques suitable for analyzing a carefully
composed human discourse apply equally to the study of nature
(Flower and Murphey 1977, 1:22-23). Edwards' idealism
enabled him to combine these concepts with traditional Puritan
typology to form a new concept of the world as a type of
spiritual realities. Perry Miller has suggested that Edwards was
reacting against the typological excesses of other Puritan
preachers, but it seems more accurate to stress the continuities
between them (Wainwright 1980, 527).

Puritan theology generally understood a type to be an event,
person or institution in the Old Testament which God designed
to foreshadow a corresponding New Testament reality. Types
are not merely tropes, for tropes are based on the inventiveness

of the human mind which uses natural objects to illustrate spiritual truth. A type, on the other hand, has a determinate and specific meaning intended by God (Miller in Edwards 1948, 1-9). A number of New England theologians extended this definition to include significant events in post-biblical history:

> By the use of typology, these men were able to read recent history, including their flight from England, as antitypes to such Old Testament events as the calling of the Israelites out of Babel.... Thus when in the eighteenth century Jonathan Edwards undertook a yet more daring extension of typology, he built upon a foundation already securely laid (Flower and Murphey 1977, 1:40).

Edwards' unique contribution to the theory of types was to declare that God has made the natural world typical of the spiritual.

> The system of created being may be divided into two parts, the typical world, and the antitypical world. The inferiour and carnal, i.e. the more external and transitory part of the universe, that part of it which is inchoative, imperfect, and subservient, is typical of the superiour, more spiritual, perfect, and durable part of it which is the end, as it were, the substance and consumation of the other. Thus the material and natural world is typical of the moral, spiritual, and intelligent world, or the city of God (Edwards 1948, 27).

In *Images and Shadows of Divine Things* Edwards customarily expresses his typological theory by stating that a natural phenomenon "signifies" or "represents" some spiritual truth. He does not mean or say that one thing simply "illustrates" another.

That the world is a typical one flows partly from Edwards' Ramist, Puritan heritage. It is also a natural consequence of his idealism. Since everything that exists has reality as an idea in the mind of God, there can be no strictly causal relationships between events in the world. All connections which appear to be based on a law of cause and effect are actually a result of

God's sovereign will. Edwards writes that, "... all oneness in created things, whence qualities and relations are derived, depends on a divine constitution that is arbitrary, in every other respect, excepting that it is regulated by divine wisdom" (Edwards 1970, 406). In his treatise on Original Sin, Edwards applies this principle to the continuity of existence of material objects as well as to the imputation of Adam's sin to his posterity (Edwards 1970, 397-412). Both are a result of God's appointment. If this is so, it is but a short step to regarding the material world as typical of the spiritual. The force which links type and antitype is not simply a natural resemblance between the two. It is the decree of God, which may even unite ideas that would not normally be conjoined. Thus, according to Edwards,

> It is a great argument with me that God, in the creation and disposal of the world and the state and course of things in it, had great respect to a shewing forth and resembling spiritual things, because God in some instances seems to have gone quite beside the ordinary laws of nature in order to it, particularly that in serpents' charming birds and squirrels and such animals [which is a lively representation "... of the Devil's catching our souls" (Edwards 1948, 45)]. The material world, and all things pertaining to it, is by the creatour wholly subordinated to the spiritual and moral world (Edwards 1948, 54).

If natural events and objects are frequently types of spiritual truth, it is reasonable to ask whether imaginary ideas of Christ might be related in some way to the true vision of Christ given to the saints. It is necessary to be careful at this point because Edwards specifically warns against the danger of using the imagination to discern the connections between the spiritual and natural worlds. "Observe the danger," he says, "of being led by fancy: as he that looks on the fire or on the clouds, giving way to his fancy, easily imagines he sees images of men or beasts in those confused appearances" (Edwards 1948, 122). However, even if imaginary ideas of Christ cannot be labeled types, may there not be some sort of connection between them and the spiritual reality they imitate; may not this connection be the result of divine appointment? Edwards' teaching on the nature of beauty suggests that it is.

Beauty and God in the World

The importance of beauty in the philosophy of Jonathan Edwards has long been recognized. The preceding pages have noted that regeneration involves a new sense or relish for God's beauty, a sense which is immediately infused in the saint by the Holy Spirit. Some aspects of Edwards' aesthetics are still under discussion—such as whether he continued to regard being as beautiful in itself (Flower and Murphey 1977, 1:153-56, 193, fn. 100). However, the major ideas are quite clear.

The most important fact about beauty in Edwards' scheme is that:

> Beauty is objective. This does not mean that beauty is in the thing if the thing is finite, for only God has beauty in Himself. Nor is beauty only in the eye of the beholder. For although Edwards traces to the eye of the beholder much that passes for beauty and much that is only limited or partial beauty, he does not accept that as the only alternative to locating beauty as an immediate property of the object. Beauty is objective in that it is constituted by objective relations of consent and dissent among beings... (Delattre 1968, 22).

Edwards' initial attempt at defining beauty begins with the notion of harmony, symmetry and proportion. The reason that these qualities involve excellency (or beauty) is that they may be resolved into equalities. Equality pleases the mind because "... disproportion, or inconsistency, is contrary to being.... But contradiction to being is intolerable to perceiving being, and the consent to being most pleasing." Edwards continues by offering "... a universal definition of excellency: The consent of being to being, or being's consent to entity. The more the consent is, and the more extensive, the greater is the excellency" ("Mind," No. 1 in Edwards 1980, 336). Primary beauty or excellence, however, cannot be found in material objects. It is located in the willing consent of minds. Such consent is nothing other than love. "Wherefore all the primary and original beauty or excellence, that is among minds, is love, and into this may all be resolved that is found among them" ("Mind," No. 45 in Edwards 1980, 362).

This concept is related to Edwards' doctrine of the Trinity. As was noted earlier, God's love and holiness are objectified in the person of the Holy Spirit. Since beauty among minds is summed up in love, the Holy Spirit is also the beauty of God.

> But he exerts himself towards himself no other way than in infinitely loving and delighting in himself, in the mutual love of the Father and the Son. This makes the third, the personal Holy Spirit or the holiness of God, which is his infinite beauty, and this is God's infinite consent to being in general ("Mind" No. 45 in Edwards 1980, 364).

Delattre has collected several other references to the Holy Spirit as the beauty of God (Delattre 1968, 152-53).

In *The Nature of True Virtue* Edwards elaborates on his theory of excellence by distinguishing more fully between primary beauty and

> ... another, inferior, secondary beauty, which is some image of this, and which is not peculiar to spiritual beings, but is found even in inanimate things; which consists in a mutual consent and agreement of different things, in form, manner, quantity, and visible end or design; called by the various names of regularity, order, uniformity, symmetry, proportion, harmony, &c. (Edwards [1834] 1974, 1:127).

Two aspects of secondary beauty are of importance for this study.

First, secondary beauty does not reside in any created object. Since the world is an ideal one and all relations are derived from God's arbitrary (though wise) decree, there is no inherent necessity that symmetry, proportion, etc. should appear beautiful. These things seem excellent because God has so ordained it. However, He has not done so without reason.

> The reason, or at least one reason, why God has made this kind of mutual agreement of things beautiful and grateful to those intelligent beings that perceive it, probably is, that there is in it some image of the true, spiritual, original beauty, which has been spoken of; consisting in being's consent to being, or the union of spiritual beings in a mutual propensity and affection of heart.... And it pleases God to observe analogy in his works, as is manifest in fact, in innumerable instances; and especially to establish inferior things with analogy to superior (Edwards [1834] 1974, 1:128).

Thus, Edwards' understanding of primary and secondary beauty is directly related to his typology. One striking example is found in gravity.

> The whole material universe is preserved by gravity or attraction, or the mutual tendency of all bodies to each other. One part of the universe is hereby made beneficial to another; the beauty, harmony, and order, regular progress, life, and motion, and in short all the well-being of the whole frame depends on it. This is a type of love or charity in the spiritual world (Edwards 1948, 79).

The second aspect of Edwards' aesthetic theory which deserves attention is based on the first. He observes that God often uses

> ... this image or resemblance, which secondary beauty has of true spiritual beauty... to assist those whose hearts are under the influence of a truly virtuous temper, to dispose them to the exercises of divine love, and enliven in them a sense of spiritual beauty" (Edwards [1834] 1974, 1:128).

Here there is none of that suspicion of beauty which frequently marked earlier Puritanism. Edwards does not use this principle to espouse the decoration of Congregational meeting-houses, but he is at least open to the concept that natural beauty can be used by God to achieve spiritual ends. Secondary beauty never leads the non-elect to a true relish for the divine beauty, but it can draw the saved person to higher experiences of God's grace. At this point, there seems to be a clear connection with Edwards' analysis of imaginary ideas of Christ. Although he describes the imaginations attending a true sense of divine things as "accidental," he does not mean that there is never any connection between the two, only that the connection is not a necessary or essential one (Edwards 1972, 238). In the same section of *Distinguishing Marks* he admits that:

> As God has given us such a faculty as the imagination, and has so made us that we can't think of things spiritual and invisible, without some exercise of this faculty, so it appears to me that such is our state and nature, that this faculty is really subservient and helpful to the other faculties of the mind, when a proper use is made of it; though oftentimes when the imagination is too strong, and the other faculties weak, it overbears 'em, and disturbs them in their exercise. It appears to me manifest in many instances that I have been acquainted with, that God has really made use of this faculty to truly divine purposes; especially in some that are more ignorant: God seems to condescend to their circumstances, and deal with them as babes; as of old he instructed his church while in a state of ignorance and minority by types and outward representations (Edwards 1972, 236).

Note that in this passage, certain exercises of the imagination are compared to Old Testament types. Both are regarded as a form of elementary instruction looking beyond themselves to a higher spiritual reality. As Edwards clearly indicated, a "... strong idea or imagination... of a person with a beautiful countenance, smiling on [someone], with arms open ..." may be a delusion of Satan (Edwards 1959, 149). However, the logical inference from the passage cited above is that such an experience may also be a perception of secondary beauty ordained by God as a pointer to the primary beauty of Christ. Thus, another aspect of Edwards' philosophy seems to undergird his willingness to treat the reported visions of converts with a measure of respect.

Retrospect and Prospect

In the preceding pages, it has been suggested that Edwards' view may have differed from the traditional Puritan appraisal of mental images of Christ. Although he regarded them with a degree of caution which often approached suspicion, he also afforded them a measure of credibility as natural concomitants of genuine spiritual experiences. Several reasons for his approach have been pointed out. These may be summarized under four headings.

Edwards' *empiricism* provided an openness to the evaluation of experience. When he found that mental images of Christ were reported by some whom he regarded as genuine converts, he was not inclined to ascribe them to Satanic agency. Second, the *psychology* which he adapted from Locke treated the human soul as a unit. Because of this the imagination could not be easily dissociated from the understanding as it sometimes had been in Puritan psychology. There was no longer room for the distinction between the "sensitive" soul and the "intellectual" soul. In addition, it became impossible to treat the new spiritual sense of the Christian as a separate faculty which could operate independently of the rest of the activities of the soul. Therefore, the imagination could be operative even during the most spiritual of experiences. Also associated with Locke's influence is Edwards' theory of *language*. An imaginary idea of Christ may be simply a sign used in thinking about Him.

In this case, it is little different than the word "Christ" which fulfills the same role. Finally, Edwards' *idealism* provided him with a view of the world in which he could develop new theories of typology and aesthetics. The relation of the physical world to the spiritual world suggests that the beauty of a mental image of Christ may (at times) function as a type of the eternal and primary beauty of God.

Although these concepts are available to the modern student, they were not all known to Edwards' contemporaries, either in New England or in Scotland. Crucial passages remained hidden in private notebooks until after his death. Treatises which were important for understanding his philosophy were not published during his lifetime, although it appears he intended them for that end. Therefore, in the Scottish controversy over imaginary ideas, it could hardly be expected that he would be understood completely. That debate is the subject of the next chapter.

Chapter 4
Mental Images: A Scottish Bombshell

The Shape of the Controversy

When Jonathan Edwards wrote Distinguishing Marks, he could not have anticipated the response it would evoke. It might have been a foregone conclusion that Chauncy would attempt a reply, but at that time the revival in Scotland existed only in the prayers of the godly. Edwards' assertion, that no one is able "... to fix his thoughts on God or Christ, or the things of another world, without imaginary ideas attending his meditations" (Edwards 1972, 236), proved to be a bombshell. However, the explosion rocked Scotland rather than New England. The spread of revival from Cambuslang and the ensuing pamphlet warfare over mental images have been sketched in Chapter Two. In the present chapter, the nature of the controversy is examined in more detail.

Slander among the Saints

Tempers are prone to rush out of control over an issue which is dear to the heart. Thus, arises the paradox of a holy truth becoming the occasion of unholy passions. In the dispute over mental images the combatants more than once give way to invective and to misrepresentation of each other's positions. James Fisher complains about the "... *manner of spirit Mr. Robe...*" displays in his various letters which are

> ... full of such invectives: and as a summary of them all, he at length tells the world, as one of his strongest arguments, that there is neither reason nor religion in that part of my Review, that concerns Mr. Edwards Sermon, "or any evidence of the knowledge of God." And yet after all he is pleased now and then to intermix the smooth words of dear Brother. I shall be sorry if it be with the same disposition as Joab spake to Amasa, 2 Sam, 20.9 (Fisher 1743, 9, preface).

Yet this same Mr. Fisher is guilty of declaring that "... the manifest *Design...*" of Edwards' *Distinguishing Marks* is

> ... to overthrow the very Foundation of Faith, and all practical Godliness, and to establish mere Enthusiasm, and strong Delusion, in the Room of the true Religion, revealed and required in the Word (Fisher 1743, 11, body).

Even the generally moderate Ralph Erskine feels it necessary to devote a whole chapter of Faith No Fancy to demonstrating "... the ignorance, error, unbelief, atheism and idolatry imported in the doctrine anent the imaginary Idea of Christ as man" (Erskine 1745, 42). Virtually all parties in the dispute could have profited from Fisher's advice given some years previously:

> Is it not a received Maxim, that no Man ought to be condemned for consequences drawn from his Doctrine, when he disclaims them?—Is it not vastly more agreeable to the Law of Love and Charity, *which thinketh no evil*, to put as favourable a Construction upon Mens Words as they can possibly admit of (Willison 1743, 8)?

One of the more serious misrepresentations deserves to be noticed at the outset of this discussion. In his *Review of the Preface* James Fisher insinuates that visions of Christ were a virtual part of the *ordo salutis* of the revival party:

> ... Mr *Edwards* acknowledges, that *this Work* is *begun by Representations* of *dreadful Objects* upon the imagination, which after violent bodily Agitations, are succeeded by imaginary or *visionary Representations*, seemingly more agreeable. . . (Fisher 1743, 13, body).

As proof of his assertion he offers a mutilated quotation from *Distinguishing Marks*:

> These that are in such Extremity (*viz.* of bodily Agony and Pain) very often have a *lively Idea* of the *horrible Pit* of eternal Misery, and at, the same Time it *appears* to them, that a *great God* who has them in his Hands, is exceeding angry with them, his Wrath appears amazingly terrible to

them, God appearing to them so much provoked, and his Wrath so incensed, they are apprehensive of great Danger, that he will *now forthwith* cut them of [sic], and send them down to the *dreadful Pit* they have *in View.*— Very many have an extraordinary Sense of their fully deserving that Wrath and Destruction, which is, *N. B. Then in their Eyes* (Fisher 1743, 13-14, body).

Webster, Willison and Robe all object to Fisher's handling of Edwards. First of all, Fisher omits phrases which make it clear that the agony and the sight of these subjects of the revival was primarily spiritual rather than physical. The "extremity" which Edwards mentions is not merely "bodily Agony and Pain" but fear of the wrath of God. Terror sometimes led to physical manifestations, but Edwards clearly notes that the work began with "... real and proper Convictions..." rather than with visions of hell (Willison 1743, 9; cf. also Webster 1743b, 9). In addition, Edwards does not seem to have visions in mind in this passage. One of the sentences Fisher omits says, "They see more and more of the vanity of everything they used to trust to ...", which clearly indicates that the kind of sight he intends is a conceptual apprehension rather than a mental image (Edwards 1972, 265). Finally, Fisher suggests that the terrible visions of the converts are generally followed by pleasant representations of Christ to their imaginations (Fisher 1743, 16). However, as the revival ministers are careful to note, Edwards specifically says that such visions, whether of horrible or of blessed objects, occurred to only a few (Robe 1743, 16).

Although there were clear distortions of fact in some of the earlier pamphlets of the controversy, these were probably not deliberate fabrications, but were rather the natural blindness which results from a zealous party spirit. However, the disturbance was not all a smokescreen. There were very real differences of opinion in crucial areas of theology, philosophy and biblical interpretation.

Substantive Issues

The majority of this chapter deals with the well-formulated positions of James Robe in his *Fourth Letter to Mr. Fisher* and of Ralph Erskine in his response to that letter, *Faith No Fancy*. Most of the concepts involved were first articulated in the early stages of the pamphlet warfare, and the arguments of the two sides continued to be developed along the lines which had been established.

Before outlining the shape of the controversy, it is important to indicate at least two areas of common ground. First of all, both sides believed in total depravity and in the necessity of a purely supernatural work of God in the new birth. In this respect, the evangelical ministers of the Church of Scotland were much closer to the Secession Church than the New Lights of New England were to some of their Old Light opponents. Second, both sides agreed on part of the definition of imaginary ideas. Robe wrote:

> Before I shew the true State of the Question betwixt you and me, allow me again to observe, That accurately speaking, an imaginary Idea, is that Idea which the Understanding formeth of corporeal Things absent from us, by the Help of the Imagination presenting the Species, or Image of these corporeal Things received and laid up in the Imagination....

All agreed, at least in principle, that imaginary ideas related only to "corporeal Things." However, Robe continued his definition by clarifying the intimate relationship which he conceived to exist between the imagination and the understanding:

> ... For, as it is not our Senses that apprehend corporeal Things present, but our Souls, by the Intervention of our Senses;—so it is not the Imagination that hath what we call the Idea of any corporeal Object absent, but the Soul and Understanding, by the Intervention of the Imagination; according to that Rule, *Oportet*

intelligentem phantasmata speculari [To perceive phantasms is necessary for understanding.] (Robe 1743, 33).

It was this connection posited between the senses and the understanding which proved to be a major target for the attacks of the Seceders.

What part do the senses play in our knowledge of the world or of God? Can an imaginary idea of Christ's human body be considered either necessary or helpful to saving faith, especially since imaginary ideas relate only to the sensible world? These issues were raised by James Fisher in his *Review of the Preface*:

> ... if there be the least *sensible* or *visionary* Representation of God or of Christ formed in our Imagination, we do that very Moment think upon a *false God* and a *false Christ*. Our Senses and Imagination, cannot assist us at all, in thinking upon the Divine Nature and Perfections (Fisher 1743, 13, body).

An important part of the question is the natural constitution of man. If it is true (as most acknowledged) "That *we cannot think upon spiritual Objects without* imaginary Ideas *attending our Meditations...*," is it because of our created nature, or is it "... owing to our lapsed and imperfect State" as Willison suggests (1743, 7)? Even if imaginary ideas attend spiritual exercises primarily because of the fall, it can be asked, "Do you think God hath created the *Imagination*, or any inferior Faculty of the Soul, merely for the Devil's Use? Hath he not Access to the *Imagination* himself when he will" (Willison 1743, 10)? Robe insists that imaginary ideas of Christ's human body are not "... a natural Fruit of Corruption...," but they arise "... from our natural Constitution, or from our finite and corporeal Nature..., and would have been as unavoidable, if we had continued in a State of Innocence as now..." (Robe 1743, 5-6). Erskine was equally adamant for the opposing view. Even if

they are unavoidable, imaginary ideas of Christ's human body
are sinful and idolatrous. At one point, he confesses with
evident shame:

> I must own and acknowledge, that, while I write upon this
> speculative subject, I am conscious to myself of so many
> vain imaginations of my own, that I am obliged to write
> against myself as well as Mr. *Robe*, and my own
> imaginary ideas as well as his (Erskine 1745, 220).

What then are the substantive issues which divide the
revivalists from the Secession ministers? First, they are
theological. Is an imaginary idea of Christ's human body helpful
to faith or is it idolatrous? Second, there are philosophical
dimensions to the problem. How is faith related to that world of
sense by which the imagination is limited? The disputants
attempted to prove their cases by appealing to approved divines
and philosophers, but they also turned to the Scriptures. The
following pages attempt to deal with these questions and with
the evidence which was offered in support of opposing
conclusions.

Theological Arguments

Claims and Accusations

When Ralph Erskine began his refutation of James Robe, he
isolated the heart of Robe's assertions in a lengthy paragraph of
his *Fourth Letter to Mr. Fisher* (Erskine 1745, 3-4). The
paragraph, which was reprinted by Erskine in its entirety, is as
follows:

> *Third* Pos. I asserted, and do assert, That we cannot think
> upon Jesus Christ really as he is, God and Man in two
> distinct Natures, and one Person for ever, without an
> imaginary Idea of him as Man, or in his human Nature,
> consisting of a true Body and a reasonable Soul.—The
> Grounds and reasons of this are, That as we would not
> have a just Conception of the glorious Mediator, if we
> have not a Conception and Idea of him, as the very true

and eternal God, as well as true and real Man; so we cannot have a just Conception of him, if we have not a Conception and Idea of him, as true and real Man, as well as the true and eternal God,—for as much as the Mediator is as really Man as he is God:—And as we ought to form no imaginary Idea of him as he is God, but a pure Conception without any Form of Representation as God in our Minds; so we can no more conceive, and have an Idea of him in our Understandings as Man, but what is called an imaginary Idea, or an Idea of him in our Minds, by the Exercise of our Imagination, than we can of *Enoch* or *Elias*, or any other Man, who is now in Heaven: For this Reason, that our Lord's human Nature, and particularly his glorified and super-exalted Body, hath all the essential Properties of any other Body, and no other;—and therefore, if we can never think of any other human Nature, or human Body, through our natural Constitution, and the Nature of Bodies, but by an imaginary Idea, when absent from us, as indeed we cannot, we can never think upon the Mediator as Man, and his Body now in Heaven, by any other Idea:—So then when we think upon the Lord Jesus Christ, as he is God and Man in two distinct Natures, and one Person for ever, I must conceive of him to be true and real Man, and this is what is called an imaginary Idea of him: I must further, by a mere Act of my Understanding, conceive of him, as not only Man, but the very true and eternal God.—And *3rdly*, I must conceive the Manhood personally united with the God-head, in the Second Person:—If any of these Three be wanting, I have not such an Idea of the Mediator God-Man, as should be.—Sir, You'll please tell the honest well-meaning People, in your next Warning, That the plain *Scotch* of what I asserted here was, that we cannot think upon Jesus Christ, as he really is, God-Man, without thinking of him as Man, as really as God, and that by the Exercise of the same Faculties and Powers, I think and conceive of other Men (Robe 1743, 30-31).

Robe clarifies the issue between himself and James Fisher by making several observations. First, all are agreed, that no one should have an imaginary Idea of Christ as God. That would certainly be blasphemous idolatry. Second, he does not teach it is acceptable to think upon Jesus Christ as a mere man, for that would imply a denial of His deity. "But the Question is, Whether our thinking of him as Man, or having an imaginary Idea of him as Man be sometimes necessary and useful and profitable to our right Knowledge of him and Use-making of him as Mediator [the God-Man]" (Robe 1743, 34). Finally, Robe denies that he makes an imaginary idea of Christ as man any part of faith. Although it does not belong to faith, yet faith cannot exist without such an idea (Robe 1743, 33-34).

Robe's denial that he is encouraging idolatry needs a little amplification. Edwards had written that "... God has given us such a faculty as the imagination, and has so made us that we can't think of things spiritual and invisible, without some exercise of this faculty..." (Edwards 1972, 236). Fisher interprets this to mean that no one can think about God without forming pictures of Him in the imagination; Robe disagrees:

> This doth by no Means follow;—for tho' we cannot think even of spiritual and invisible Things without some Exercise of Imagination, and some Help from it to the other Faculties, yet this is not by the Imagination's presenting any imaginary Form or Picture of them:—This is not the Use of the Imagination about spiritual Things, which are nowise the Object of this Faculty (Robe 1743, 8-9).

Robe explains that the imagination helps the superior faculties to conceive of God by presenting to them images of sensible objects which God in His Word has made to be signs of divine truth. For instance, water is a symbol of the Holy Spirit, who is invisible; an imaginary idea of water presented to the understanding helps the mind to conceive of how the Spirit refreshes a weary soul.

> From all this you see it clear as the Sun, that the Imagination may be useful to the other Faculties, to think upon spiritual and invisible Things, without conveying Ideas of them unto the Mind, by imaginary Forms or Pictures of them (Robe 1743, 10).

Robe reinforces his position by an appeal to Edwards' comparison of the imagination to Old Testament types. As types were not pictures of God, so (Robe concludes) the imaginary ideas discussed by Edwards in this passage were not of God or of other invisible things (Robe 1743, 10).

However, Robe insists that an imaginary representation of the human body of Christ is not an image of God. Therefore, it is not idolatrous. Neither does it have to contain all of the details which would be included in a picture of Christ.

> For it is not required to a Conception or an imaginary Idea of Christ as Man, that I conceive or have an imaginary Idea of his Body, of such a Stature, of such Proportion and Lineaments, as were the exact Stature, Proportion and Lineaments of the Body of Jesus Christ...; an universal Idea, applied to the Particulars, with other Circumstances taken in by the Imagination or Understanding, as the Nature of the Thing requires, being all that is needful here (Robe 1743, 40).

Therefore, an imaginary idea of Christ as man is not necessarily a vivid picture in the mind. It may be a rather generalized notion of what is involved in constituting a human body.

Erskine disallows Robe's distinction between imaginary ideas as a help to faith and as a component of faith. Therefore, he treats imaginary ideas of Christ's human body as idolatrous:

> For there is no difference between Christ considered only as a human creature, or a corporeal object, (as Mr. *Robe* speaks) and any other human creature, or corporeal object, as such, which may be seen or viewed by the eye or fancy in a natural way without sin; But to be viewed or thought of in a religious way, so as to make that any part of the object of faith or religious worship, is as monstrous idolatry as ever was among heathens... (Erskine 1745, 11).

... it is impossible and unlawful, yea atheistical and idolatrous, to have (what Mr. *Robe* calls) *an imaginary idea of the human nature of the lovely Jesus.* Indeed these very words appear, in my view, to smell rank of idolatry; as if the loveliness and beauty of Christ's human nature did consist in anything perceptible by an imaginary idea: Whereas it is truly impossible to perceive the real and true loveliness of Christ, by any mere natural and unrenewed faculty (Erskine 1745, 150).

The claims of James Robe and the accusations of Ralph Erskine reveal attitudes that are poles apart. It seems surprising that two evangelical ministers from the same theological heritage could come to such diverse opinions. What were their reasons?

Robe's Arguments

James Robe outlines his defense of imaginary ideas of Christ under three headings. First, he writes, "... we may warrantably have an Idea or Conception of either of the Natures of Christ, and think upon either of them, without thinking upon, or having an Idea of the other at the same Time..." (Robe 1743, 53). In the same way, it is possible to think of God's eternity without a simultaneous conception of His omnipotence. Such a separation of ideas does not divide God into distinct parts, and it is not sinful. It is merely a natural consequence of human finitude that we cannot think of many different things at the same time. Second, thinking of Christ's manhood by means of an imaginary idea does not exclude a belief in His being more than man. Erskine assumes the two are mutually exclusive, but Robe expresses abhorrence at the notion (Robe 1743, 53-54).

Robe's third heading is slightly more complex. He attempts to prove that imaginary ideas of Christ are definitely helpful to faith. His major thesis is that a true idea of the Mediator is a complex idea consisting of three distinct ideas—an idea of Him as man, an idea of Him as God, and an idea of Him as God and man together. An idea of Christ's humanity includes an idea of His body, and no one can have an idea of Christ's human body without forming an imaginary idea of it. He illustrates his meaning with a "Similie."

> Man consists of Soul and Body,—the Soul, being a spiritual Substance, is not conceived by any imaginary Idea; but the Understanding must conceive of it by a simple and pure Act of its own:—But the same Understanding conceives of the Body, when out of Sight by an imaginary Idea, which cannot extend unto the Soul; and yet that imaginary Idea, tho' it can extend no further than the Body, is not only helpful, but necessary to think upon any particular Man; because we can have no Idea of the whole Man without it (Robe 1743, 55).

In other words, an imaginary idea of Christ as man is a psychological necessity based on the way human beings think.

Early in his argument Erskine points out a glaring inconsistency in Robe's terminology. Robe frequently writes about an "imaginary idea of Christ as man" or even an imaginary idea of Christ's "human nature". Robe explicitly limits imaginary ideas to corporeal objects. However, the human nature of Christ contains more than His body; it also includes, according to the Larger Catechism, "a reasonable soul" (Question 37). Therefore, he leaves himself open to Erskine's gibe that "sound divines" have never understood the phrase "Christ as man" to refer merely to Christ's human body (Erskine 1745, 12).

This criticism is not fatal to Robe's position. He could have avoided reference to "an imaginary idea of Christ as man" or to an imaginary idea of Christ's "human nature." It would have been sufficient for his purposes to say that an imaginary idea of the human body of Christ is necessary for the understanding to meditate on His human nature. That, however, would not have touched the more crucial issues. According to Erskine:

> If Mr. Robe had spoke of the imaginary idea of Christ as a human body, instead of saying, as man, it would have been more tolerable philosophy; because the corporeal idea and the corporeal object would agree. But still it would have been intolerable divinity... (Erskine 1745, 45).

Erskine's Arguments

The "intolerable divinity" of Mr. Robe is the encouragement he gives to idolatry. Mental idolatry is just as real a threat as mental adultery.

> If a man shall frame an imaginary idea of a woman in his mind, to lust after her, it is mental adultery. Even so it is mental idolatry, to form a picture of Christ's human nature in our mind by an imaginary idea of it; and so to make that the object of faith or worship.... Indeed I know not who can justify themselves, and say, they are free of this sin in some measure. It is too natural to every man... (Erskine 1745, 49).

Erskine's analysis of mental idolatry attempts to be thorough. His position may be arranged in a logical sequence from basic premises to a strong conclusion.

Erskine's fundamental proposition is that "God only is the proper object of faith and worship. The human nature of Christ is not God. Therefore, the human nature of Christ in itself, is not the proper object of faith and worship" (Erskine 1745, 48). Much less can an imaginary idea of Christ's body be the object of faith or worship, since it is not even the whole of His human nature. However, Robe makes the imaginary idea of Christ as man to be necessary to faith. Therefore, it is a part of faith and as such constitutes idolatry. Robe grants all of these statements except the conclusion. As noted earlier, he emphatically denies that an imaginary idea of Christ as man is a part of faith. In order to undermine Robe's position Erskine must demonstrate that an imaginary idea of Christ is not necessary to faith and then show that it is positively dangerous to faith.

Consider first whether imaginary ideas are necessary to faith. Robe admits that the understanding conceives of God without utilizing an imaginary idea of Him. Moreover, the complex idea of Christ as the God-man is formed in the understanding rather than in the fancy (Robe 1743, 54). On the other hand, the imagination cannot judge truth or falsity by itself. It can only present pictures to the mind without passing judgment on their validity.

> But if, when the understanding comes, it can conceive justly enough of Christ as God-man in one person, which is a *whole Christ*, why must he still discredit his understanding, as if it could not manage that matter without the help of that ignorant act, which is destitute of understanding, and can help no farther than to present the picture of a man in the head, under the name of Christ... (Erskine 1745, 196).

Consequently, Erskine maintains (in opposition to Robe) that imaginary ideas are under the control of, the will. Robe urges that pictures and statues are voluntary creations, but that an imaginary idea of Christ as man is an involuntary production of the imagination whenever the mind is meditating on the historical accounts of Christ's life, death and resurrection (Robe 1743, 45). Erskine, however, insists that the imagination forms images passively only during dreams and under exceptionally strong motions of the "animal spirits." Otherwise its image forming ability is active and is governed by the will. Therefore, "vain imaginations" of God or Christ can be and are expressly forbidden in Scripture, and imaginary ideas are not necessary to a believing apprehension of Christ (Erskine 1745, 158).

The next logical stage of Erskine's argument is to demonstrate that imaginary ideas of Christ as man are dangerous. He objects to making an imaginary idea the foundation of all thinking about Christ because that is

> ... to conceive of him in a sense wherein he is neither a God, nor a person... The subject wherein that humanity exists, being his *divine person*, which cannot be the object of any imaginary idea; to begin therefore to think of Christ by an imaginary idea of him as man, is to begin with Atheism, or with a thought that necessarily excludes his Deity, and cannot include it; because Christ as man cannot be God. Therefore, as long as he uses that first help, namely, an imaginary idea of him as man, he brings himself under a necessity of denying that he is God... (Erskine 1745, 78).

Furthermore, any picture of a man, whether external or internal, necessarily supposes a human person as the subject of the image. Therefore, Robe is guilty of encouraging Nestorianism, or the doctrine that Christ has two persons (human and divine) as well as two natures (Erskine 1745, 46). Erskine notes that the early church faced the problem of those who argued it was possible to make an image of God after the incarnation because Christ as man may be figured or pictured. The seventh synod, though unrecognized by the Roman Church, charged image making with Nestorianism because it "... separated the human nature from the divine" (Erskine 1745, 292). As Erskine summarizes the issues:

> The image then... must either represent a human person, or a divine one. If the *image of Jesus Christ* he speaks of, represent a *human person*, then it is not the true image of Christ, who never had, and never was a human person; and so it conveys nothing but lies and falshoods. If the image of Christ he allows of, represents a *divine person*, then it is the image of God; for Jesus Christ is God, the second person of the glorious Trinity: And, consequently, whether Mr. *Robe* will or not, it is but an idolatrous picture of him who is God, expressly forbidden in the second command (Erskine 1745, 155-56).

The final stage of Erskine's argument is to demonstrate how Christ's human nature may be the object of faith without involving an imaginary idea of Him as man. His answer is "... that the human nature of Christ is the object of faith in all the properties of it, as they are recorded and asserted in the word" (Erskine 1745, 304). Propositional truths are not the objects of fancy, so these may be believed without an imaginary idea of Christ as man. Erskine gives a number of examples of the kind of truths which he intends, including: Christ's miraculous birth, the purity and holiness of His human nature, the union of the divine and human natures in one person, the anointing of the humanity of Christ with the Holy Spirit, and the exaltation of the man, Christ Jesus (Erskine 1745, 297-312). Prior to this Erskine has argued that imaginary ideas are voluntary, unnecessary, and harmful to faith. In showing how faith in Christ's human nature may exist without them, he has justified his claim that mental images of Christ are idolatrous. They are not God's appointed means for apprehending the humanity of the Savior. However, it may still be asked whose opinions are "orthodox," Robe's or Erskine's? What do the learned (and approved) divines say? That question was still very important in the first half of the eighteenth century.

Theological Sources

It is significant that both James Robe and Ralph Erskine turn to Puritan tradition for support. This in itself suggests that the tradition was not uniform, but the question of the preponderance of testimony may still be raised. The argument from history began very early in the controversy. Adam Gib in his *Warning against... Mr. George Whitefield* cites the famous *Parable of the Ten Virgins Opened and Applied* by Thomas Shepard:

> Some . . . have heard *Voices*, some have seen the very *Blood* of Christ *dropping* on them, and his *Wounds* in his

Side; some have seen a great *Light* shining in the
Chamber, some wonderfully affected with their *Dreams*;
some in great *Distress*, have had *inward* Witness, *Thy
Sins are forgiven*; and hence such *Liberty* and *Joy*, that
they are ready to *leap* up and down the Chamber.—Wo to
them that have no other manifested Christ, but *such* a one
(Gib 1742, 61).

Although Gib uses this quotation as evidence that the
revival converts were "... *exposing* themselves to *satanical*
Influence..." (Gib 1742, 61), two observations need to be made.
First, Shepard's description is essentially the same as Edwards'
account of some subjects of the revival (*vide supra*). Second,
the crucial phrase in Shepard's condemnation is "no other
manifested Christ." Is it possible for such an experience to
coexist with true faith, or are they mutually exclusive? That is
the point in dispute, and it is not resolved by the quotation.

Both parties continued to search their libraries, and some
months later James Fisher is still insisting that the divines
quoted by Mr. Robe "... grant that imaginary ideas of God, are
ready to attend our meditations of him, in this state of
imperfection, yet they expressly condemn these ideas as the
fruit of a corrupt imagination" (Fisher 1743, 11-12, preface,
original italicized). In response John Willison states that there
is no difference between Edwards or Robe and the most
respected authors of earlier days—he mentions Flavel and
Charnock (Willison 1743, 7).

With this background of controversy Robe's *Fourth Letter*
and Erskine in *Faith No Fancy* clearly address the question of
theological antecedents to their positions. Since both Robe and
Erskine accuse each other of minimizing the true humanity of
Christ, many of the quotations which they produce are designed
only to delineate the orthodox doctrine of the incarnation.
Thus, not all of them are really apposite to the subject of mental

images of Christ. One of Robe's favorite sources is Stephen Charnock,

> ... where speaking of this very Subject, *imaginary Ideas...* where shewing, that we must by no Means conceive of God under a human or corporeal Shape,—He saith, "We may indeed conceive of Christ as Man, who hath in Heaven the Vestment of our Nature, and is *Deus figuratus*, tho' we cannot conceive the Godhead under a human Shape" (Robe 1743, 36).

Again Charnock, discussing the sufferings of Christ writes,

> Here we may see the Sufferings of his Body, his Pains upon the Cross; and here *Fancy* may work about the unconceivable Troubles of his Soul.—Here *Fancy* may represent the piercing of his Temples by the Thorns, and the Dints made in his Body (Robe 1743, 45).

Erskine's attempts to deal with these quotations are awkward at best. He admits that

> . ... this way of speaking would never be my choice. . . yet I am persuaded, *Charnock* would never have expressed himself in such terms as these, if he had thought his words would have been interpreted, as Mr. *Robe* does, in favours of Imaginary ideas of mere corporeal things .... And it appears, as I said above, that *Charnock* here must understand some other thing by fancy, than Mr. *Robe* means by an imaginary idea; because he speaks of fancy working about the inconceivable troubles of Christ's soul (Erskine 1745, 162).

It is true that Charnock speaks of the troubles of Christ's soul, but he also mentions the sufferings of His body. If it be objected that the fancy (according to Robe's definition) cannot picture the soul, yet it is also true that Robe himself is not entirely consistent in his usage, when he writes about an imaginary idea of Christ as man. Therefore, a slight inconsistency in terminology should not be used to avoid the natural force of Charnock's words.

In order to pull the sting from Robe's citations, Erskine offers another from Charnock:

> "The vision of Christ in his glorified human nature, is a seeing of God face to face. So that whosoever sees Christ with his bodily eyes, or with the eyes of his mind, sees God; he sees and knows God, not immediately and directly, but mediately and consequently." I see [comments Erskine] no passage could have been so pat for Mr. *Robe* as this: And yet it will not quadrate with his doctrine, relating to the imaginary idea of Christ as man, that is, of his human body; because, when *Charnock* here speaks of seeing God in the face of Christ, he means the person of Christ. . . (Erskine 1745, 136-37).

Since a sight of the *person* of Christ is, according to Erskine, totally outside the scope of the fancy, Charnock cannot be interpreted to intend an imaginary idea of the Savior's body. Erskine's assessment of these passages is less than convincing. On the other hand, Charnock may not be addressing the question of vivid mental images directly. Nevertheless, his expressions at least provide Robe with an opportunity for claiming theological precedence for his views.

Another significant author whom Robe paraphrases is Turretin (Robe 1743, 44). Erskine provides a more precise citation in order to dispute with Robe's conclusions. Turretin writes:

> Ab *imagine mentali* ad *imaginem sculptam vel pictam* non valet consequentia; quia ilia est necessitatis, siquidem conspicere non possum rem ullam sine aliqua specie ejus, aut idea in animo efficta. At imago ista conjuncta semper est cum spiritu discretionis, quo verum a falso ita secernimus, ut nullum sit idolatriae periculum. Sed ista meri arbitrii & voluntatis opus, quod a Deo expresse est prohibitum, & quod magno cum idolatriae periculo semper est conjunctum. Unde perperam non minus peccatum dicitur imagines certarum rerum menti objicere, vel scriptis comprendere, & legendas exhibere, ac eas in tabula delineatas visui subjicere; cum magnum sit inter ista discrimen.

[The conclusion drawn from a mental image to a sculpted or painted image is not valid, for (a mental image) is necessary, since it is not possible to consider anything without some representation or idea of it having been produced in the mind. Moreover, such an image is always joined with a spirit of discretion, by which we distinguish truth from falsehood, in order that there may be no danger of idolatry. But (a picture or a sculpture) is a purely voluntary work, which is expressly forbidden by God, and which is always joined with great danger of idolatry. Therefore, it is wrongly said that there is no less sin in holding images of certain things before the mind or in perceiving them in books and exhibiting them to be read, than in presenting them to the sight drawn on a tablet, although there is a great difference between such things.] (Erskine 1745, 367).

Erskine objects that Robe has misrepresented Turretin in several ways. Two are worthy of mention. First, Robe's paraphrase includes the words, "... whereby we separate that which is true from that which is false, that there is no Danger of Idolatry" (Robe 1743, 45). Erskine notes that the subjunctive *sit* has not been translated properly

> ... as if he had said, *there is* no danger of idolatry; whereas he plainly supposes the danger... But he mentions... a spirit of discerning, whereby... we *may* avoid that danger. Hereby that learned author intimates, that whatever false representation is made to the mind of the true spiritual worshipper, is altogether involuntary, and such as, by the help of that spiritual discerning which is given to him, he rejects and drives away from him, that he may not worship an idol... (Erskine 1745, 368).

This observation is technically correct, but it misses the point. Robe's citation of Turretin is still valid as a witness that certain kinds of mental images of Christ are not as reprehensible as external ones. In addition, Turretin states that such images are involuntary, a fact which Erskine attempts to use, but which is directly contrary to his principles.

Second, Erskine supposes that the mental image mentioned by Turretin is not equivalent to Robe's imaginary idea since Turretin is referring to intelligible objects, which may be read about in books, rather than to images of sensible objects, such as the human body of Christ (Erskine 1745, 368-69). However, what Erskine neglects to notice is that sensible objects described in books may engender vivid mental images in the reader. Again, it appears that Robe has found an ally whose expressions are at least suitable for the use he makes of them.

Even more appropriate for Robe's purpose is this selection from Looking unto Jesus, a work by Isaac Ambrose which has frequently been reprinted, even through the nineteenth century:

> But thy Jesus was crowned with Thorns, and sceptred with a Reed, and that Reed was taken out of his Hands, to beat the Crown of Thorns into his Head; and besides, thy Jesus was whipped with Cords, and Rods, and little Chains of Iron, that from his Shoulders to the Soles of his Feet, there was no Part free; and being now in this Plight, thou art called to behold the MAN: Dost thou see him? IS THY IMAGINATION STRONG? Canst thou consider him at present, as if thou hadst a View of this very Man (Robe 1745, 45)?

Again, Erskine is at a loss to deal properly with such expressions. He seems unwilling to slander a name he honors, so he extends a hand of "charity" to Ambrose and reinterprets each of his damaging expressions in a manner opposite to their natural sense. Finally, he concludes that "If this were not his meaning,... then, though he had been an angel of light, his doctrine was to be rejected as carnal, and not spiritual" (Erskine 1745, 162-63).

Erskine is on much stronger ground, however, when he produces his own quotations from learned authors who oppose mental images of Christ. His lengthiest selections (extending for over seven pages plus other material interspersed throughout the rest of the chapter) come from one of the most eminent of Puritan divines, John Owen. Two of these quotations are reproduced below:

> Many there are who, not comprehending, nor being affected with that divine spiritual description of the person of Christ which is given us by the Holy Ghost in scripture, do feign unto themselves false representations of him by images and pictures, so to excite carnal and corrupt affections in their minds. By the help of their outward senses, they reflect on their imaginations the shape of a human body, cast into postures and circumstances dolorous or triumphant; and so, by the working of their fancy, raise a *commotion* of mind in themselves, which they suppose to be love unto Christ. But all these idols are *teachers of lies*. The true beauty and amiableness of the person of Christ, which is the formal object and cause of divine love, is so far from being represented herein, as that the mind is thereby *wholly diverted* from the contemplation of it: *For no more can be so pictured unto us, but what may belong unto a mere man, and what is arbitrarily referred unto Christ, not by faith, but by corrupt imagination. The beauty of the person of Christ as represented in the scripture, consists in things invisible unto the eyes of flesh. They are such as no hand of man can represent or shadow. It is the eye of faith alone that can see this King in his beauty.* What else can contemplate on the uncreated glories of his *divine nature?* Can the hand of man represent the union of his natures in the same person, wherein he is peculiarly amiable? What eye can discern the mutual communication of the properties of his different natures in the same person which depends thereon, whence it is that God laid down his life for us, and purchased his church with his own blood? In these things, O vain man! doth the loveliness of the person of Christ unto the souls of believers consist; and not in those strokes of art which fancy hath guided a skilful hand and pencil unto. And what eye of flesh can discern the inhabitation of the Spirit in all fulness in the *human nature?* Can his

condescension, his love, his grace, his power, his
compassion, his offices, his fitness and ability to save
sinners, be decyphered on a tablet, or engraven on wood
or stone? However such pictures may be adorned,
however beautified and enriched, they are not that Christ
which the soul of the spouse doth love; they are not any
means of representing his love unto us, or of conveying
our love unto him. They only divert the minds of
superstitious persons from the Son of God, unto the
embraces of *a cloud composed of fancy and imagination*
(Erskine 1745, 314-315).

This is that glory whereof we ought to endeavour a
prospect by faith; *by faith*, I say, *not by imagination.*
Vain and foolish men, having general notions of this glory
of Christ, knowing nothing of the real nature of it, have
endeavoured to represent it in pictures and images, with
all that lustre and beauty which the art of painting with
ornaments of gold and jewels can give them. This is that
representation of the present glory of christ [*sic*], which,
being made and proposed unto the imaginations and
carnal affections of superstitious persons, carries such a
shew of devotion and veneration in the *Papal* church. But
they err, not knowing the scriptures, nor the eternal glory
of the Son of God. The glory that the Lord Jesus Christ is
in the real, actual possession of in heaven, can be no
otherwise seen or apprehended in this world, but in the
light of faith, fixing itself on divine revelation. *To behold
this glory of Christ, is not an act of fancy or imagination.
It does not consist in fancying to ourselves the shape of a
glorious person in heaven. But the steady exercise of
faith on the revelation and description made of this glory
of Christ in the scripture*, is the grand rule and measure of
all divine meditations thereon. Every pretence of a desire
of heaven, and of the presence of Christ therein, that does
not arise from, that is not resolved into that prospect
which we have of the glory of Christ in this world by faith,
is mere *fancy and imagination* (Erskine 1745, 316).

The important feature of these quotations is not that they
clearly separate an imaginary view of Christ from saving faith.
Both Edwards and Robe do that. What is significant is that they

so utterly exclude any positive value from such representations to the fancy. In addition, Owen implies that any who entertain imaginary ideas of Christ are strangers to the grace of God.

Shorter excerpts are given by Erskine from a number of lesser Puritan lights. Some of them deal with such subjects as the hypostatic union, the place of the affections in relation to the understanding, and the general subject of idolatrous images of God without touching directly on the subject of the fancy. One of the authors who deals directly with mental idolatry is Thomas Boston in his evangelical classic, *Human Nature in Its Four-fold State*. Boston writes:

> Doth not the carnal mind naturally strive to grasp spiritual things in *imagination*; as if the soul were quite immersed in flesh and blood, and would turn everything into its own shape? Let men who are used to the forming of the most abstracted notions, look into their own souls, and they shall find this bias in their minds: Whereof the idolatry which did of old, and still doth so much prevail in the world, is an uncontestable evidence. For it plainly discovers, that men naturally would have a *visible Deity*, and *see* what they worship: And therefore *they changed the glory of the incorruptible God into an image made like to corruptible man*, &c. Rom. 1.23. The reformation of these nations (blessed be the Lord for it) hath banished idolatry and images too out of our churches: But heart-reformation only can break down *mental* idolatry, and banish the more subtile and refined image-worship, and representations of the Deity, out of the minds of men. The world in the time of its darkness was never more prone to the former, than the unsanctified mind is to the latter. And hence are horrible, monstrous, and mishapen thoughts of God, Christ, the glory above, and all spiritual things (Erskine 1745, 325).

Here Boston identifies all imaginary thoughts of spiritual things with an unsanctified mind. They can hardly be considered as potential signs of deepening spiritual conviction. He does not merely discourage imaginary ideas of Christ; he condemns them.

A final example of the attitude of the pious toward mental images is given by Mr. James Fraser of Brea. In his frequently reprinted treatise on justifying faith he writes of

> ... such as come to, and close with a Christ and idol of their own fancy; and it is thus: When men hear tell of Christ, the idolatry of the *carnal mind* doth presently form a kind of carnal image of Christ in its own fancy, and falls down and worships, and believes this idol thus fancied, *Hos.* xiii. 2. *Acts* xvii. 29.—Their imagination formeth some idea of him, to what the *idolatrous* carnal mind doth assimilate him; which idea is all they have for Christ. Verily, when Christ is externally revealed, there must be a glorious light to discover Christ, as he is in himself; which light is from God alone, and a supernatural work, and the beginning of all saving differencing good, and which discovers Christ to the soul really.... Whereas this idolatrous apprehension of Christ, is a mere dead fancy, and is lifeless, (like external idols;) doth *not transform the soul into the same image*, nor humble, nor rejoice the soul, but the soul continueth in the same case it was (Erskine 1745, 326).

Considering the variety of witnesses adduced by both Robe and Erskine, it is fair to ask whether there existed a Puritan consensus regarding mental images of Christ. Part of the difficulty is indicated by Erskine as he commences his survey of the literature available to him:

> Though I know of none that ever directly treated on this subject, and I know not if ever any had occasion to do so till now, that such strange doctrine is introduced and intermixed with divinity; yet there are many instances of incidental discourses, ...or occasional testimonies in the writings of divines, against all imagery, internal as well as external, in religion. Some of the instances suitable, I think, to the present subject, are these following... (Erskine 1745, 312).

The great respect accorded to the Westminster standards among Presbyterians, Congregationalists and Calvinistic Baptists (who all adopted forms of the Confession) suggests that there was something of a consensus on basic principles. The 109th question of the Larger Catechism lists among the sins forbidden by the second commandment "... the making any representation of God, of all or of any of the three persons, either inwardly in our mind, or outwardly in any kind of image or likeness of any creature whatsoever...." Puritan authors, including those cited above, frequently denounced mental idolatry and saw in it the evil source of all external image worship. James Robe, by his own admission, stands within that tradition. However, the controversy which began in 1742 appears to be the first attempt to define precisely the limits of mental idolatry. When do the natural and unavoidable mental symbols by which men think become idolatrous? That is the question.

Although there is room for disagreement, it appears that Ralph Erskine stands within the conservative mainstream of tradition, while James Robe is stretching its borders. Erskine is certainly harsher than some of his predecessors when he condemns all mental imagery of spiritual things. However, the expressions which seem so congenial to Robe's position may not have been intended to include the vivid imaginary ideas which Robe defends. Since this is an issue affecting Edwards as well, further confirmation of the Puritan position on images is given in chapter five.

Robe blurs the distinction between the normal symbols used in thinking and vivid mental images. That blurring is a natural result of the traditional definition of the imagination, which includes both kinds of experience under the same faculty. When early Protestants adopted Scholastic forms of thought (in spite of warnings from some of the Reformers), they inherited a number of problems. Among these was a potential conflict between their understanding of the imagination and the rejection (by some groups) of mental images of God. Since the medieval Church embraced all kinds of images, no such conflict was possible for it. The Cambuslang revival provided a stimulus for focusing attention on the problem, but it does not seem that either Robe or Erskine recognized that their differences stemmed from inherent inconsistencies in the traditions of reformed scholasticism.

Philosophical Arguments

In addition to the theological debate over idolatry, there is also considerable discussion of the philosophical differences between the revival party and the Seceders. Unfortunately, a great deal of energy is expended on issues of little or no importance. Philosophical quibbles abound. Two examples will suffice. Robe charges James Fisher with "… ignorant and blundering Nonsense…" because he calls "… an imaginary Idea, a sensible Representation upon the Imagination" (Robe 1743, 25). The imagination provides representations of sensible objects to the understanding when those objects are absent. The representations are not "sensible" because the senses are not producing them at the moment they are recall ed. Therefore, Fisher should have put "… INTELLIGIBLE REPRESENTATION, for SENSIBLE REPRESENTATION of sensible Objects…" (Robe 1743, 26).

Ralph Erskine is guilty of the same kind of cavil. In order to prove that an imaginary idea of Christ as man is not foundational to a belief in His humanity, he analyzes the sentence "Christ is man." "Christ" is the subject, "man" is the predicate, and "is" constitutes the copula which links the two together. A "… common rule of natural philosophy…" teaches that a knowledge of the subject is logically prior to a knowledge of what is predicated about it. Robe is charged with inverting this order, "For, to make the first thing here, in order to believe that Christ is man, to be an imaginary idea of Christ as man, is, to suppose that *man* is the *subject*, and Christ the *predicate*; which none that have common sense, will aver..." (Erskine 1745, 62).

The substantial issues which separate the two parties deal with the nature of the human soul and the manner in which men come to know about the world outside themselves. The twin disciplines of psychology and epistemology dominate much of Erskine's critique of Robe. To these subjects, it is now necessary to turn.

Erskine contra Locke

Ralph Erskine was well acquainted with the philosophy of John Locke. Erskine's treatise evinces an interesting acceptance of some of Locke's terminology, and an even more striking rejection of his fundamental tenets. Consider the following discussion of ideas:

> Simple ideas are these that come into our mind by sensations; as, colors by the eye, sounds by the ear, etc. Complex or compound ideas are founded by the power which the mind hath of comparing, separating, or extracting its simple ideas, which come into it by sensation and reflexion (Erskine 1745, 5).

This is almost parallel to Locke's treatment of how the mind deals with simple ideas:

> 1. Combining several simple *Ideas* into one compound one, and thus all Complex *Ideas* are made. 2. The 2*d*. is bringing two Ideas, whether simple or complex, together; and setting them by one another, so as to take a view of them at once, without uniting them into one; by which way it gets all its *Ideas* of Relations. 3. The 3*d*. is separating them from all other *Ideas* that accompany

them in their real existence; this is called *Abstraction*:
And thus all its General *Ideas* are made (Locke 1975, 163).
Erskine, however, has no admiration for Locke.

> I am so jealous of the danger professed Christians are in,
> of losing their way in the thickets of Pagan philosophy,
> from which they borrow many dangerous maxims, but I
> would not chuse even that way of speaking which is very
> common among some Christian philosophers, *viz*. of
> sensation and reflexion, as the fountains of knowledge,
> *Locke* on *human understanding*, &c. from whence they
> say all ideas we can naturally have, do spring (Erskine
> 1745, 114).

The pagan philosopher whom Erskine principally has in
mind is Epicurus. He sees dangerous parallels between the
empirical philosophy of Robe and Locke and the atomistic
materialism of Epicureanism (Erskine 1745, 98-99, 268-70). He
takes exception to Robe's rule, "... *Oportet intelligentem
phantasmata speculari* [To perceive phantasms is necessary for
understanding]" (Robe 1743, 33). To this he opposes the dictum
of the "... great philosopher *Hiereboord... Mens non indiget
semper phantasmatis ad suas perceptiones* [The mind does not
always require phantasms for its comprehensions]" (Erskine
1745, 99). As a corollary to Robe's rule, Erskine suggests
another which

> ... seems to be equally espoused by his doctrine; and as
> necessary to support his principle anent the *senses* as this
> to support his principle anent *imaginations*: The rule is,
> as elsewhere mentioned, *viz. Nihil est in intellectu quod
> non fuit prius in sensibus*; that is, *Nothing is in the
> understanding that was not first in the senses...* (Erskine
> 1745, 107).

Erskine opposes empiricism because he wishes to make
room for innate knowledge, a subject to be discussed below. In
his determined rejection of Locke and Robe, he sometimes
makes statements which seem extreme. For example, in
contradistinction to Robe's rule, he proposes one of his own:

"*Oportet intelligentem phantasmata supprimere, subvertere, subruere* [To suppress, overthrow and tear down phantasms is necessary for understanding]. . ." (Erskine 1745, 128). Or consider his even more striking assertion that "The sight of the object itself, does not help the faculty of seeing" (Erskine 1745, 277). The basis for such statements is found partly in the older faculty psychology (which Erskine continued to accept in place of the newer teaching of John Locke) and partly in more recent philosophical developments in France and the Netherlands.

The Independence of the Faculties

The great difference between Locke and Erskine is that Erskine divorces sensation from the understanding, while for Locke sensation and reflection are the fountains of all knowledge and understanding. In general, Erskine follows the psychology of his Puritan forebears. It does not seem to trouble him that there was no unanimous opinion among them; the separation and independence of the faculties was held by most of them, at any rate. Richard Baxter, quoted by Erskine, summarizes the situation:

> But in these things even Christian philosophers differ. 1. Some think, man hath three distinct souls, intellectual, sensitive and vegetative. 2. Some that he hath two, intellectual and sensitive; and that the vegetative is a part of the body. 3. Some, that he hath but one, with these three faculties. 4. Some, that he hath but one with these two faculties, intellectual and sensitive. 5. Some that he hath but one, with the faculty of intellection and will; and that the sensitive is corporeal. (So little do we know ourselves).—What I think most probable I have opened *jn methodo theologie*; That man hath but one substantial soul, with both intellectual and sensitive faculties; and that it is uncertain whether the vegetative be its faculty, or only the faculty of the igneous or ethereal substance which is the immediate vehicle of the soul. It is enough for us to know as much of our souls as our duty in using them and our felicity, doth require; as he may know his clock,

watch, house, horse, who knows not how to make them, nor can anatomize them (Erskine 1745, 7-8).

In addition to the separation of the natural faculties, Erskine teaches the "... necessity of saving illumination, and of supernatural faculties for apprehending supernatural things" (Erskine 1745, 197). These faculties are nonexistent in the unregenerate man. In one of his clearest passages on the subject he writes:

> Sense, imagination, and understanding, have been distinguished in philosophy, by the following example. When we behold the sun with open eyes, then external *sense* is manifest; when we shut our eyes, and think upon the sun, then internal sense or *imagination* is manifest. But, when we consider the apparent distance, and compare the apparent magnitude or bulk of the sun, with what must be the real distance and real bulk of it, then *understanding* is manifested.... Sense, reason and faith are powers and faculties that act in their own proper spheres, as different in themselves, as the first, second and third heaven. *Sense*, whether external or internal, (as above mentioned), hath for its object things corporeal; *reason*, properly, things intellectual; and *faith*, things spiritual and supernatural, revealed in God's word. Sense cannot aspire to the sphere of reason, nor reason to the sphere of faith; and far less can sense and imaginary ideas do so (Erskine 1745, 10).

Elsewhere, he reinforces the principle of the separation of the natural and spiritual faculties with a quaint illustration.

> The body is helpful in its own place for bodily things; but not properly for spiritual. Our feet, for example, are greatly helpful to our walking upon the earth; but are not therefore greatly helpful for walking upon the sea. If a man, by a miraculous power, were enabled, with *Peter*, to walk upon the water, surely he could not do so without feet; because, whatever element one may be said to walk upon, suppose fire, water, earth or air, while we are in the body, we cannot walk otherwise but with our feet: But will

it follow therefore, that our feet are great helps to us to walk upon the water; because, properly speaking, we cannot walk at all without feet, but, go where we will in the body, must take our feet along with us. Even so our bodily senses and imaginations attend our most spiritual actings; but they can no more help us to walk in these spiritual paths, or help us to saving knowledge and faith, than our feet can help us to walk on the face of the deep, on the head of a cloud, or on the top of a rainbow (Erskine 1745, 256).

Erskine offers several proofs for the independence of the faculties. In order to show that the imagination is not helpful to the understanding he demonstrates that dumb animals have imaginary ideas even though they do not have an intellect. A dog shows that he has an imaginary idea of his master "... by seeking after him, and distinguishing between him and thousands of other men in a crowd" (Erskine 1945, 68-69). An imaginary idea of Christ as a man affords, by itself, no greater knowledge of Him than a beast might have. Furthermore, the imagination has no capacity for judging between what is true and what is false. That capacity belongs to the intellectual faculty. An imaginary idea of Paul presents only the outward form of a man, but it does not produce faith in the statement that Paul was an Apostle. Some things which may be described are not credible because they cannot be imagined, for instance, a mountain without a valley. However, other things, such as a golden mountain, may be imagined without being credible. The reason is that imagination relates only to the faculty of sense, but credibility is determined by the reasoning faculty. Much less, therefore, can imagination assist faith; imaginary ideas of the human body of Christ cannot be helpful to faith in Him as the God-man (Erskine 1745, 71-74).

The crowning argument for the independence of the spiritual faculties is given in answer to a gibe from James Robe.

Robe insists that the natural faculties are necessary to the saving knowledge of God because "... all the Knowledge of God, his Nature and Perfections, we have by the outward Means of his Works and Word, which the Holy Spirit makes effectual, is attained by the Intervention of our Senses and Imagination" (Robe 1743, 61). He challenges Erskine to prove

> ... that the natural essential Powers God hath given to us as Men, are not helpful to us; but we would know God much better if we wanted them:—That is to say, a Man would attain the Knowledge of God's Nature and Perfections, by the visible Things of the Creation, much better, [if] he were blind, deaf, without feeling, and the other Senses, and without the Faculty of the Imagination (Robe 1743, 63).

Erskine replies,

> ... That though God's people were blind and deaf, and destitute of other bodily senses, and of the imaginative faculty of fancying and framing images of bodies; yet they would know God much better without these bodily organs, as it is with departed souls, than if they had them all, and yet wanted rational souls; as it is with brute beasts (Erskine 1745, 259).

The body is a burden to the soul, and Scripture teaches that it is far better to depart these houses of clay and to be with Christ. Therefore, though the senses may give occasion for the soul to think upon God, they are by no means necessary for that purpose.

In Erskine's attack against empiricism, he not only attempts to destroy the connection which Robe posits between the senses, the intellect and faith; he also defines his own doctrine of the relation of the natural faculties to each other and to the spiritual faculties. The result is neither Cartesian skepticism about the reliability of the senses nor Locke's utter dependence upon them.

Erskine's Epistemology

Erskine finds the foils for placing his own views in a proper perspective within the ancient schools of the Skeptics and Epicureans. He intimates, without identifying them completely, that the modern representatives of these philosophies are the Cartesians and the followers of John Locke. At least tendencies toward the folly of the ancients are present in modern philosophers. Erskine deliberately steers a middle course between the two extremes. Robe, he declares, seems to alternate between these two errors. His doctrine of imaginary ideas appears to be roughly parallel to the Cartesian's dependence on innate ideas, but his insistence on the senses as the foundation of knowledge borders on Epicureanism. On the whole, Erskine concludes, the danger of Epicurean heresy is the more imminent (Erskine 1745, 265-69).

Erskine summarizes his own middle way in four propositions. First, some principles of truth are inborn; they are "connatural" to all men. These include basic presuppositions necessary to logic and mathematics and the recognition "... That there is such a thing as natural body, motion, place, time, &c." Second, the senses may be trusted to give accurate information regarding the sensible world. When men are deceived regarding such things, it is the judgment, not the senses which err. Third, objects of sense "... may be occasions, arguments and confirmations of faith..." even though they are not properly helps to faith. Obvious examples are creation and miracles as evidences of God's power and the sacraments which speak of God's grace. Fourth, there is a close connection between the soul and the body so that "... the rational soul can scarcely think of any thing, unless the forming of the conception be occasioned by some sensation" (Erskine 1745, 266-7).

In order properly to understand Erskine's doctrine it is necessary to distinguish between innate ideas (which he disallows) and innate knowledge, which is essential for knowing God or the world. Innate ideas, as explained by the Cartesians and the Platonists, consist of "... images, representations, intelligible species of all things, in the mind..." which are "... divinely ingenerate in us; as if whatsoever is in this life learned more perfectly, were but a certain mere remembrance of or calling to mind what was once in the mind before..." (Erskine 1745, 272,276).

In order to illustrate and prove his doctrine of innate knowledge, as distinct from innate ideas, Erskine turns to the father of the human race. Adam

> ... knew God in his relative being, as his God and friend; otherwise he would never have fled away from him with shame, when the friendship was broken by his sin. He knew God before ever he knew the creatures, for he was created after God's image, in knowledge, righteousness and holiness, with dominion over the creatures. He knew God in these things of God which the creatures could not teach him, namely, the mind and will of God as to his duty; for he had the perfect knowledge of the law of God, which was written on his mind, and concreated with him (Erskine 1745, 273).

For Erskine, as for most Puritans, the ultimate proof of Adam's innate knowledge is seen in his naming the creatures.

> Even as *Adam* (as I said) could not know the creatures to give them their names, suited to their nature, unless he had got that knowledge from the God of nature given to him before ever he saw them; thus it is with us: Though we have lost such a knowledge of God as thereby to know the creatures, and such a knowledge of the creatures, as to give them all their names according to their natures; yet so much of this knowledge remains, that whenever we see them, then we know them, in some respects to be what they are, and that this, or such a creature is distinct from

such an other, because we had this knowledge before (Erskine 1745, 276).

Because of the fundamental importance of innate knowledge to Erskine's system, one further illustration of his meaning seems justified:

> Whether this be called *subjective* light, consisting in our ability to perceive, discern, know and judge of objects, as contradistinct from *actual* knowledge, or whether it be called *innate* knowledge, in contradistinction from acquired, or whatever name else it may come under; I take this to be the *fountain*, route and spring of all *acquired* knowledge; of which none are capable that want this seed, this faint remains of the Divine image: So faint, so small, so languid, that I may suppose it like the tender smoke of a candle, when both flame and fire is extinguished; yet the remaining fume or smoke when brought within the reach of any other fire or flame, doth natively catch it, even at some distance; so as to set it a-burning and flaming again; which it could not do, if there were no remains at all of the fire and flame about it. Such is the native power and aptitude of that remaining heat and smoke to exert itself, as long as the igneous particles have life and motion, which, whatever fire approaches, is naturally prompt and ready to receive it. Thus it is here: So low and deeply buried under the rubbish of corruption our natural knowledge of God is, that this candle of the Lord within us is, as it were, quite extinguished both as to the fire and flame, and nothing remains but some little heat and smoke; which yet has so much of the nature of knowledge as to be capable, or apt to receive and take hold of the light that approaches to it, This I call *innate*, and suppose to be so much the root and source of *acquired* knowledge, that none at all could be acquired without it. And, to ascribe knowledge to external causes, without this presupposed, to me, appears a denying, so far, the divine original of the light of nature (Erskine 1745, 114-15).

A full explication of Erskine's philosophy requires that his separation of the faculties be related to his doctrine of innate knowledge. Erskine distinguishes several objects of knowledge. First is the knowledge of natural things for which innate knowledge of the creature is necessary. Without this it is not possible to process the information which comes through the senses. Second, God implants a natural knowledge of Himself in the human heart ". . . which, as *Mastricht* says, arises from *the very Being of God coexistent with the understanding....*" Such knowledge must be distinguished from the natural knowledge of God which is occasioned by observation of nature. However, none of this encompasses the saving knowledge of God. The reason is that all natural knowledge is contained in the intellectual faculty. In order to go beyond this, there must be a new kind of innate knowledge implanted in the soul, a new faculty to receive a new kind of knowledge. The same principle holds both in nature and in grace. "If God should manifest himself to us, before we have his image restored, we could not know him: He must first *give us an understanding to know himself*, I John v. 20" (Erskine 1745, 278-79).

Erskine's refutation of Robe is now complete. Against Robe's declaration that the senses and imagination are helpful to faith, he argues that the faculties are so separate that an apprehension of corporeal objects cannot assist and may hinder intellectual comprehension of Christian doctrine. In addition, no degree of natural knowledge can take the place of supernatural illumination and the creation of supernatural faculties for receiving that light. Finally, the true source of actual knowledge, whether in nature or in grace, is innate knowledge implanted directly by God. The senses may give occasion for improving the understanding; they cannot inform it. Thus, according to Erskine, imaginary ideas of Christ's human body are to be rejected. They present the threat of mental idolatry, and their supposed usefulness is based on poor philosophy. But whose philosophy is being propounded?

Neither Erskine nor Robe claims to be original. What, then, are the sources of their philosophy?

Philosophical Sources

The basic issue for which Robe and Erskine seek support is the relationship of the senses to the acquisition of knowledge. Robe cites several passages from two well-known Puritan divines to prove that the knowledge of God depends on the senses and the imagination.

> *Burges* upon *Original Sin*, Page 351. "The imaginative Power or Phantasy in a Man, is immediately subservient to the Understanding in its Operations." Page 353 "The imaginative Faculty is so near to the Intellectual, that in all its Operations, it (*viz.* the Understanding) hath some Dependence upon it."

> *Manton*, Vol. III. Page 32. "God hath given us a Body, bored through with five Senses to let out Thoughts, and to take in Objects; to taste the Goodness of God in the Creatures, and see Divinity in them, and hear the Voice by which they proclaim the Glory of God. Page 53. Meditation upon the Creatures is a Work that is of great Profit; partly to heighten Fancy, and make it fit for Meditation. O practice upon the Creation, and you will find Fancy to be much elevated and raised."—Page 256. "Mans Reason is lower than that of the Angels, because it needs the Ministry of *Fancy* and *Imagination*, Fancy needs *outward Sense*, which an Angel needeth nor" (Robe 1743, 61-62).

Robe rounds out his citation of Puritan worthies with a reference to an earlier quotation from Charnock:

> While we are in the Body, and surrounded with fleshly Matter,—something of Sense will interpose itself in our purest Conceptions of spiritual Things; for the Faculties which serve for Contemplation, are either corporeal, as the Sense and Fancy, or so allied to them, that nothing passes into them but by the Organs of the Body (Robe 1743, 8).

Erskine deals with all these citations in a similar manner. He attempts to show either that the references have nothing to do with the saving knowledge of God or that the senses involved are spiritual rather than physical. He next argues that though the intellect may be dependent on the exterior senses, the senses are not properly helpful to it (Erskine 1745, 241-248). His favorite technique for doing this is the *reductio ad absurdam*. Consider the following example:

> I might here observe, that the air we breathe in, is subservient to the life of the body, hence also to the support of the corporeal faculty of sense and fancy, which Mr. *Robe* makes so greatly helpful to bring us to the saving knowledge of God; why then, the air we breathe in, is at least immediately subservient, or a remote help to the saving knowledge of God. And at this rate our daily eating and drinking, and sleeping to support the bodily frame with its sensitive faculties, or any thing subservient to sustain the frame of nature, may be brought in as greatly helpful to the saving knowledge of God (ibid., 244).

It must be judged that Erskine does not deal fairly with the evidence adduced by Robe. He does not acknowledge that the authors cited may have held a different epistemology than his own, and he does not adequately show that their views are the same as his. Erskine is, however, able to find learned men to support his cause. One such divine is John Flavel:

> The fancy indeed, while the soul is embodied, ordinarily and for the most part, presents the appearances and likeness of things to the mind; but yet it can form thoughts of things which the fancy can present no image of; as when the soul thinks of God or of itself.... We deny (says he) that the soul knows nothing now but by phantasms and images: For it knows itself, its own nature and powers, of which it cannot feign or form any image or representation.... To understand by species, (says he,) does not agree to the soul naturally and necessarily, but by accident, as it is now in union with the body.... So that,

to speak properly, the body is bettered by the use the soul makes of it in these noble actions; but the soul is not advantaged by its being tied to such a body. It can do its own work without it; its operations follow its essence, not the body to which it is for a time united (Erskine 1745, 104-5).

As a matter of fact, the role of the senses in the acquisition of knowledge had been hotly debated in the century preceding the revivals. While Erskine makes occasional use of British divines, such as Flavel, he relies most heavily on three Dutch philosophers to demonstrate his epistemology. They are Gerhard de Vries, Peter van Mastricht, and Adriaan Heereboord—spelled Hiereboord by Erskine. In order to evaluate Erskine's debt to the Netherlands, it will be helpful briefly to trace the development of Cartesianism in the seventeenth century. Throughout this discussion, it should be remembered that the label "Cartesian" does not imply, either in Erskine or in other writers of the period, that the positions of Descartes himself are accurately described or actually adopted.

In 1629 René Descartes left his native France to settle in the Netherlands. Within a few years, the university faculties at Leiden and Utrecht were polarized into opposing camps over the new philosophy. At Leiden, Aristotle was officially mandated for the curriculum by Curators of the University, but in practice Cartesian doctrines were often taught with impunity. Heereboord has been identified as one of the proponents of Cartesian philosophy at Leiden, but he was actually more an eclectic than a close follower of Descartes. Nevertheless, he played a central role in the o early disputes over Cartesianism. An indication of his influence in reformed circles may be seen from the fact that his *Meletemata Philosophica* was used as a natural philosophy text at Harvard as late as 1740 (Wallace Anderson in Edwards 1980, 12). In 1650 Johannes Cocceius joined the faculty at Leiden. Although he cannot be clearly called a Cartesian himself, his followers became known as disciples of the new philosophy. Tensions continued to increase until in 1656, and again in 1676, matters reached crisis proportions. On both occasions the Cartesians suffered setbacks, primarily for political reasons. In 1673, before the issue had reached a head, Gerhard de Vries, a member of the philosophy faculty at Leiden, complained to the Curators about persecution from Cartesian students and professors. Although he was offered an increase in rank and salary, he refused to stay. Instead, he accepted a position at Utrecht which had, for nearly forty years, been dominated by the strong personality of Gisbert Voetius, a leader of the opposition against both Descartes and Cocceius (McGahagan 1976).

In the ecclectic epistemology of Heereboord, Ralph Erskine finds an ally for his proposition that not all knowledge comes through the senses. Heereboord "... combined traditional Aristotelian doctrine with the empiricism and utilitarianism of the New Science...." However, he "... did not completely reject the Cartesian way of ideas, but confined it to knowledge of the self and of spiritual things, which were the only objects which could be known without conversion to the phantasm" (McGahagan 1976, 225-26). As noted earlier Erskine cites him against Robe's rule, "*Oportet intelligentem phantasmata speculari.*" A more detailed discussion of Heereboord's position is given by Erskine in the following words:

> Thus this same learned author shews, how the *understanding acting by phantasms,* is true only with reference to things sensible and external, not with reference to things spiritual and invisible: With respect to which he proves the following position, namely, *That all understanding is so proper to the soul even in this life, that not only hath it no dependence upon the phantasy, as upon the efficient and subject thereof, but also hath*

sometimes no dependence upon the phantasy or phantasm, as upon the object or occasion thereof; and instances the knowledge that the soul may have of God and angels, and of itself: And then he refutes the error of those who assert, that the understanding hath no perception of spiritual things, God, angels, or of itself, but by analogy of things corporeal, and according to material objects formed in the fancy... (Erskine 1745, 100).

True Aristotelians were often not ready to grant Heereboord's exceptions to empirical knowledge. The controversy may be approached by focusing on the corollary to Robe's rule which Erskine imputes to him, *"Nihil est in intellectu quod non fuit prius in sensibus*; that is, *Nothing is in the understanding that was not first in the senses..."* (Erskine 1745, 107). This maxim rests on the Scholastic view of perception according to which the essential form of a material thing is transmitted through some medium to make an impression on the sense organ.

The Scholastics then require that the phantasm formed by Imagination contain as abstractable the essential form or intelligible species of the thing to be known. For the Scholastics, what is known is not something which simply belongs to the knower; the intelligible species *is* the essential form of the thing known shared by the knower. But in the Cartesian account, the idea which arises is only a modification of the mind, which is not the same as, nor even essentially like, the known thing's form as the Cartesians understand it.... [U]pon the Scholastic account of perception the significance of the maxim, *Nihil est in intellectu quod non prius fuerit in sensu*, is apparent. If material things did not act through a medium upon the sense organs, nothing would be known" (Watson 1966, 7).

The necessity of the senses for understanding could be, and was carried to its logical conclusion by some philosophers. For instance, Samuel Maresius, a French Calvinist immigrant to the Netherlands, in his support for Aristotelianism "... defends the proposition *Quod non est in sensu, non est in intellectu* even with respect to the doctrine of God…" (Bizer 1965, 67). By the 1740s few people were taking seriously the old Scholastic epistemology. Newton, Locke and others had made radical changes in men's comprehension of the physical universe. However, the old Scholastic dictum could be defended on the grounds of the newer empiricism which was taking shape. This, apparently, is the route traveled by James Robe.

Although he was an opponent of Heereboord and, for the most part, a follower of Aristotle, Voetius at least agreed that the knowledge of God was innate. Voetius is not quoted by Erskine, but his conclusions regarding atheism seem to be mirrored in Erskine's distinction between an innate idea and an innate knowledge of God. It has often been assumed that Voetius' charge of atheism against Descartes was merely a "cheap shot" designed to raise popular suspicions. However, McGahagan demonstrates that the allegation resulted from deeply held convictions. In his inaugural theses at Utrecht (1634) Voetius maintained "… that 'there are no speculative atheists, who are certainly persuaded that God does not exist, and that it was not possible to completely extinguish our innate knowledge of God." His reason for defending such a position rests on his opposition to the "… Socinians and Remonstrants, who held that we have no knowledge of God save that revealed in Scripture, and that it is therefore impossible to formulate dogmatic propositions which go beyond the explicit words of Scripture" (McGahagan 1976, 154-155).

Descartes, it is true, spoke of an innate idea of God, but this idea had to be drawn out through rational arguments; it did not constitute actual knowledge. On the other hand, Voetius taught that since our innate knowledge of God is the knowledge of Him as creator, it can only be elicited through observation of the creature. The senses are necessary, and various arguments (especially from causality) are helpful, but only because they serve to remind us of the knowledge of God which we already have (McGahagan 1976, 156-57).

How, then, can there be any true atheists? Voetius' answer is that though there are no speculative atheists, there are many practical atheists. Practical atheism is a moral defect by which men deny the knowledge of God which is theirs at birth. Thus, any disobedience to the will of God is an obscuring of the law of God written on the heart; deliberate doubt of God's existence is a sinful denial of the innate sense of God which is given to all men. Such doubt cannot be excused on the grounds that it paves the way for a more certain proof of God's existence because the rationalistic proof used by Descartes is too obscure for many to follow and because it is never acceptable to do evil that good may come. Thus, the class of practical atheists includes not only Cartesians, but "... Deists, heathens, Jews, Moslems and sectaries..." (McGahagan 1976, 159). McGahagan notes that Calvin also

> ... emphasized that the moral sense of God which was innate was distinct from any purely philosophical notion of God, and related to obedience to the law of God rather than to philosophical speculation....

> ... Voet was more faithful to Calvin than his scholastic language... might indicate. For Voet as well as Calvin, atheism was a moral rather than an intellectual issue. Voet's disciple Hoornbeek... noted that only papist authors such as Gassendi used "idea" for our notion of God, and that Calvin preferred to speak of an innate "sense" of the divine (McGahagan 1976, 205-06).

After the death of Voetius in 1676 the campaign against the Cartesians was waged by another Utrecht philosopher, Peter van Mastricht (McGahagan 1976,53). Erskine refers to his anti-Cartesian works a number of times, in one lengthy citation, offered for the benefit of the "learned," Mastricht explains how it is possible to know that God exists.

Porro 3. distinguendum quoque hic existimamus inter rei
existentiam & ejusdem *essentiam*: adeoque licet res
quoad suam *essentiam* non possit esse intellectu quin
fuerit in sensibus; omnino videtur asserendum attamen,
rei *existentiam* posse esse in intellectu, quae nunquam
fuerit in sensibus. Quamvis enim formae substantiales
(loquor ex hypothesius Peripateticorum, de quorum effato
hic agitur) quoad *essentiam* seu *quidditatem* suam non
sunt in intellectu nostro, quia nunquam fuerunt in
sensibus; attamen quoad *existentiam* seu *quodditatem*
(barbarismis scholasticis Cartesiani sunto, quaeso,
propitii) omnino sunt in intellectu: quamvis enim nesciat
intellectus quid sit forma canis, bovis, asini, a parte sui,
novit tamen ex effectis, cani, bovi, adesse suam formam
substantialem prorsus ad eundem modum quo ex fumo
colligo *existentiam* seu praesentiam ignis, quamvis ipsam
hujus ignis essentiam nec sensus nec intellectus
perceperit. Plane eodum modo quamvis *essentiam* seu
quidditatem Dei intellectus noster non percipiat, eo quod
numquam fuerit in sensibus attamen *existentia* seu
quodditas Dei ex creaturis per sensus omnino colligitur, &
a sensibus ab intellectu percipitur, eo quod effectus
infallibiliter arguat existentiam suae causae secundae
justa & primae.

[We also consider it necessary in this matter to
distinguish between the existence of a thing and its
essence: moreover, it is granted that a thing is not able to
be in the intellect, as far as its essence is concerned,
unless it has been in the senses. Nevertheless, it certainly
seems it must be declared that the existence of a thing
which was never in the senses is able to be in the intellect.
For although the substantial forms... are not in the
intellect as far as their essence or whatness is concerned,
because they have never been in the senses, nevertheless,
as far as their existence or thatness is concerned... they
certainly are in the intellect. For although the intellect
does not know what the form of a dog or a cow or an ass
may be from a part of it, nevertheless, it knows from the
effects, with respect to a dog or a cow, that its substantial
form is present, in absolutely the same way as I conclude

from smoke the existence or presence of fire, although the essence itself of this fire neither the sense nor the intellect perceives. In the same way although our intellect does not perceive the essence or whatness of God distinctly because it has never been in the senses, nevertheless, the existence or thatness of God is certainly concluded from the creatures through the senses, and from the senses it is perceived by the intellect, because the effect proves infallibly the existence of its supporting cause to be nearby and first.] (Erskine 1745, 233-34).

Therefore, when Erskine insists that a sense or knowledge of God is innate and that this knowledge is only evoked by the senses, he is able to rest his case on a strong, although not universal, Protestant tradition. Erskine cites Anthony Burgess' summary of the situation: "But that which the Protestant authors hold is, That [a man by the light of nature] may indeed have the knowledge, *that* there is a God; but *what* this God is, whether he be one, and what his attributes are, they cannot so reach to..." (Erskine 1745, 233). There was a consensus among non-Cartesian Protestants that the senses play some role in man's natural knowledge of God. But what is that role? Are the senses channels through which the knowledge of God comes, as Robe (in line with part of the Aristotelian tradition) insists? Or do the senses merely help the mind to remember what it already knew before, as Erskine (following the Voetians) concludes? Further insight into Erskine's position, known as "occasionalism," may be derived from a brief glance at the difficulties experienced by French Cartesians during the late seventeenth century.

Cartesianism collapsed as a coherent system because of irreconcilable contradictions in its basic assumptions. Descartes posited the existence of two created substances, mind and matter. These were assumed to be totally unlike each other. He further accepted the traditional view that effects must be like their causes and that direct acquaintance is necessary for knowledge. Finally, he taught that sensations and ideas are only modifications made on the mind by interaction with external objects through a medium. In spite of this, ideas represent external objects to the mind, while sensations do not.

Simon Foucher leveled several criticisms at these tenets. First, causal interaction between mind and matter is impossible if these are different substances. Therefore, since mind and matter do interact, they must have some likeness of essence. In addition, the mind cannot have direct acquaintance with an external object if its sensations and ideas are only mental modifications. If sensations cannot represent external objects, neither can ideas. Both arise from the same source. Therefore, knowledge of the world is impossible. However, we do appear to have some knowledge of the world; therefore, Cartesianism must be false (Watson 1966, 29-39).

Faced with such attacks, philosophers found that several options remained open. Baruch Spinoza, for example, solved the problem of dualism by positing the existence of only one substance, God. Mind and matter were assumed to be modifications of that one substance (Watson 1966, 105-06). Later, John Locke attempted to make the way of ideas more intelligible, but in so doing kept most of Descartes' problems and added a few of his own (Watson 1966, 107-11). The "orthodox" Cartesians maintained a strict dualism between mind and matter but insisted that interaction between the two does take place. This they were able to do because they denied the likeness principles, "... that likeness is necessary between cause and effect, and that likeness is necessary between what represents and what is represented" (Watson 1966, 89). Therefore, interaction between dissimilar substances ceased to be a problem. (Watson suggests, however, that the attempt to divest themselves of the likeness principles was unsuccessful and that this caused the downfall of their system.) Finally, some thinkers, of whom Nicholas de Malebranche was the most prominent, chose the alternative of occasionalism.

Malebranche accepted the dualism of Descartes as well as both likeness principles. He denied, however, that mind and matter interact. God is the intermediary who connects the regularly occurring sequences which we are accustomed to denote by the term, "cause and effect." Occasionalism may be illustrated as follows:

> ... when, for example, I will to move my arm, that is the occasion for God to make my arm move, and when an object is in my field of vision, that is the occasion for God to produce a visual appearance in my mind.... God's causal intervention is required even for one billiard ball to move another. God is the one true cause, and it is solely due to his providence that regularities in experience occur (Shaffer 1967, 342).

God's direct action describes not only how the mind moves the body; it also explains man's knowledge of the world. Malebranche accepts the definition of sensations as mental modifications, but he teaches that ideas are not modifications of the knowing mind. Rather they are imparted directly by God who had to have ideas of material objects before He created them (Watson 1966, 99).

The occasionalism of Erskine bears a strong resemblance to that of Malebranche, with one major exception. Erskine sometimes admits that knowledge of the physical world comes more directly through the senses. His occasionalism is more consistent with reference to spiritual objects. It is the knowledge of God which he is especially concerned to preserve separate.

There is, however, no indication that Erskine derived his occasionalism directly from Malebranche. A number of other thinkers arrived at similar conclusions, and Erskine's clearest stated source is de Vries.

> The foresaid author [de Vries], I say, speaking of incorporeal things, declares, that bodies, or corporeal things give occasion, and only an occasion, to conceive of them; Which occasion the mind could not make use of, so as thence to proceed to the thoughts of incorporeal things, unless it could think of incorporeal things in an incorporeal manner. And though the thoughts of spiritual things may so far depend upon sense, as that it may furnish occasions of forming them; yet, for the phantasms of these spiritual things, (as all objects of faith are) to be exhibite to the mind, is of itself directly oposite [sic] to the very nature of things (Erskine 1745, 101-02).

In other words, the nature of a spiritual object is obscured by the very phantasm which is supposed to be a help in perceiving it. The Latin text of the preceding quotation, cited by Erskine in a footnote, concludes with the caution:

> Atque hinc apparet, quo modo limitandae veniant, ut sint verae, vulgares regulae [Hence, it is also apparent in what way these common rules, which are accepted as true, must be limited]: *nihil est in intellectu, quod non ante fuerit in sensu: Oportet intelligentem phantasmata speculari, &c*] (Erskine 1745, 102).

The limitation is that they do not apply to spiritual objects, but the implication, stated elsewhere, is that they do apply to material ones.

What, then, can be concluded about the philosophical background of Ralph Erskine and James Robe? First of all, it was mixed, and that very lack of uniformity allows both men to appeal to their common traditions for support. Second, as noted earlier, neither Erskine nor Robe seems willing to concede the existence of these differences. Third, Erskine is probably closer to the mainstream of Puritan tradition in his insistence that some knowledge of God is innate. Robe does not appear to deny this explicitly; perhaps the arguments based on

Adam's knowledge of God and the animals were too strongly imbedded in his background to dispute. Finally, however, Erskine's occasionalism is a more novel answer than he recognizes. Many of the sources he cites to prove innate knowledge or the independence of the soul from the senses do not directly deal with this aspect of the problem. Shaffer states that, "Occasionalism is an inherently unstable theory that seemed plausible only for a moment in the history of philosophy, as a desperate attempt to maintain Descartes's system despite the internal conflict between his two-substance doctrine and his concept of causality" (Shaffer 1967, 342). Erskine is trapped by the problems of Cartesianism even as he struggles against it.

Win, Lose, or Draw

In eighteenth century Scotland, there was no neutral panel of judges to determine whether Ralph Erskine or James Robe had won their debate. Even if there had been, the results might have been doubtful. Certainly, both parties scored points, but neither adequately addressed all of the necessary issues. If the vote may be said to have been cast by the Scottish people, even here results were mixed. In the years immediately following 1743, God continued to bless both the Secession Church and the evangelical ministers of the Church of Scotland. Harvests were not as plentiful as during the revival, but the ground was not barren either.

Perhaps the best way to evaluate the controversy is to consider the points upon which the disputants agree. It is then possible to ask which of them best adheres to the common terms of the debate. Both parties accept the principle that external or internal images of God are idolatrous. Our ideas of God must not be attended by any mental pictures of Him. Both also accept the traditional definition of the imagination as the image-producing faculty of the mind. They differ on whether an imaginary idea of the human body of Christ should be considered idolatrous. Robe's doctrine would be more defensible if he were content to state that such ideas are completely neutral events with purely psychological explanations. His insistence that imaginary ideas of Christ's human body are helpful and necessary to faith places the matter in a far more unfavorable light from the traditional perspective. In order to provide a better defense of his orthodoxy, Robe should state clearly when, if ever, a mental image of Christ would be idolatrous. His own account of his pastoral dealings in such cases demonstrates that he discouraged any reliance on imaginary ideas, but it also suggests that he did not warn his people of the danger of idolatry at the same time. Robe's handling of this important theological issue appears to be weaker than Erskine's.

On the other hand, Erskine's declaration that propositional truths are not the objects of fancy is open to serious question. He believes he has found a way to conceive of Christ as man without the aid of imaginary ideas of corporeal objects. However, it is difficult to think of the virgin birth without imagining a woman and a baby. Even a notion of the purity and holiness of Christ's human nature depends on physical analogies. To think of purity usually involves the recollection of other things which are "pure"—the whiteness of snow or the brightness of sunlight, for example. True, such images do not constitute idolatry; they are not representations of the Divine Being. However, Erskine is not willing to grant the senses so large a role in man's knowledge of God. In his eagerness to destroy Robe's reliance on the fancy, he also undermines the notion that men think by means of symbols. However, he does not seem to be aware of this problem. Perhaps his rejection of all imagery in thinking of spiritual objects is a case of philosophical overkill.

If the results of the debate are thus far somewhat indeterminate, there still remains one authority from which there is no appeal. Both Robe and Erskine acknowledge the absolute supremacy of the Bible. Part of their correspondence relates to Edwards' incidental omission of the word "sole" when referring to the authority of Scripture (Erskine 1743, 45-46; Robe 1743, 64-66). It might be expected, therefore, that careful exegesis of Scripture would undergird their efforts to establish the truth regarding imaginary ideas. As a matter of fact, that is not the case. Since both agree that images of the living God are sinful, there is no need for establishing that principle on the basis of biblical texts. Other areas of difference prove less amenable to scriptural demonstration. The attempt is, of course, made. In most cases, dogmatic eisegesis determines the outcome. The texts discussed by Erskine and Robe cover three potential helps to faith—the body of Christ, the body of the Christian, and the testimony of creation.

The Body of Christ

In *Fraud and Falshood* Erskine asserts that imaginary ideas of Christ's flesh and blood are equivalent to knowing Him after the flesh. He then asks,

> If such Views do natively and necessarily attend our Faith while we ourselves are in the Flesh, and have Flesh as well as Spirit about us; yet are not these carnal Views the greatest Lets and Contradictions, instead of being Helps and Advantages to Faith, or any part of it? Does not Christ forbid such carnal Notions of *eating his Flesh, John* vi.? Such Fancies and gross Imaginations made his Hearers there to stumble at the true Christ; therefore he says to them, v. 65 [*sic*, v. 63], *It is the Spirit that quickneth, the Flesh profiteth nothing; the Words that I speak unto you, they are Spirit and they are Life.... If the Flesh profit*

nothing, what a vain Imagination is the View of an absent Man, or a fanciful thinking... (Erskine 1743, 49-50).

Robe, naturally, complains that Erskine has perverted the words of Scripture. He notes that, "This is their plain and only Meaning,—to eat Christ's Flesh only as the *Capernamites* understood him, can profit nothing, either to the Comfort of the Soul, or the Resurrection of the Body" (Robe 1743, 56). It may be granted that there is no reference in John 6 to imaginary ideas of Christ. However, Robe's further cavil is certainly wide of the mark. He charges Erskine with making the blasphemous denial that the humanity of Christ is profitable.

The issue is not whether the Lord's humanity is necessary for his work as Mediator, but whether a perception of his physical body is profitable for salvation and faith. Erskine not only attempts to prove that an imaginary idea of Christ is harmful. He also implies approval of the judgment that seeing, Christ on earth "... was a very great hinderance [*sic*] and obstacle to faith" (Erskine 1745, 226). The risen Lord forbade Mary to touch Him because her conceptions of him were still carnal (John 20:17). However, the woman with an issue of blood genuinely touched Christ by faith even though she only made contact with the hem of His garment (Luke 8:44-46). The multitude which pressed in on the Lord had a surer touch of His body than she, but that did not give them faith. As a further illustration of this principle, Erskine notes that the Apostles' imaginary idea of 1oaves did not help them to believe Christ could supply bread (Erskine 1745, 224-29). The obvious answer to such examples is that they only prove that the physical presence of Christ did not necessarily produce faith. They fail to show that faith may have been hindered by His presence.

More to the point is Erskine's reference to John 16:7.

> If his removing from his disciples as to his bodily
> presence had been a disadvantage to faith, then it would

> never have been *expedient for them, that he should go*
> *away*: But he has told us the expediency thereof, because
> of the Spirit of faith, his coming to fill up that room to
> advantage. The absence of Christ as to his human nature
> is no hinderance [sic], but rather a furtherance to faith;
> because the person of Christ, the God-man, is as much
> present to faith, as if his human body were on earth, in
> our sight and in our arms; in which case, we might be
> ready to mistake, and think we saw and embraced the
> person, while, instead thereof, we would only see and hug
> the human body of Christ by sense (Erskine 1745, 226).

However, in this passage Jesus is not stressing the benefits of
His absence, but the importance of the coming of the
Comforter. The coming of the one was dependent on the going
of the other. Is not Erskine's interpretation a virtual denial of
the significance of Christ's earthly ministry? Was it to no
purpose that He allowed Himself to be handled by sinners?

In this connection, one passage which is not noted by either
Robe or Erskine cries out for recognition:

> What was from the beginning, what we have heard, what
> we have seen with our eyes, what we have looked at and
> touched with our hands, concerning the Word of Life—
> and the life was manifested, and we have seen and testify
> and proclaim to you the eternal life, which was with the
> Father and was manifested to us—what we have seen and
> heard we proclaim to you also, so that you too may have
> fellowship with us; and indeed our fellowship is with the
> Father, and with His Son Jesus Christ (1 John 1:1-3).

It appears that Erskine's only line of defense against this text
would be to say that the seeing and handling are not merely
physical because no one can determine that Jesus is the Word
of life by mere contact with His human body. True enough, but
to separate John's sensible apprehension of Christ from his
spiritual perception of the incarnation virtually deprives the
passage of its meaning. This conclusion is reinforced by noting
that part of John's purpose in the epistle is to prove that Christ

has come in the flesh (I John 4:2-3). The prologue provides a personal testimony to the truth of his message. If Erskine is concerned about the practical atheism of the Cartesians, perhaps it is not amiss to suggest that he may himself be leaning toward a practical Docetism. Although Robe does not use the term, that is the thrust of much of his criticism of Erskine.

The Body of the Christian

The second aspect of the scriptural argument addresses the issue of whether men would be able to know God better without their bodily senses than with them. The mere suggestion seems ridiculous to Robe, and he doubts whether many of the Seceders will want to deprive themselves of their sight, hearing, etc. in order to put Erskine's conclusions to the test (Robe 1743, 63). Erskine denies that he or his friends would deliberately do themselves harm, but they would sometimes hope for God to shorten their earthly pilgrimage.

> For I must tell Mr. *Robe*, there are even among the Seceders that would heartily chuse sometimes to be out of the body, and all its senses that God hath given to it, that they may know him better than they do; and who would chuse, not only to be quite free of a body of sin and death, but also of burdensome bodies of clay too, with all the darkening glasses they now see him by, that they may see him face to face, and know as they are known, 1 *Cor.* xiii. 12. and that they may be like him, by seeing him as he is, 1 *John* iii. 2. This was the exercise of the saints in scripture, 2 *Cor*, v. 1,2,3,4. *Phil.* i. 21,22,23. and it hath been, and sometimes is the exercise of some of these whom Mr. *Robe* mocks as Seceders (Erskine 1745, 260).

Unfortunately, Erskine seems to be evaluating the body more from a Greek than a biblical perspective. In one of the texts cited, the Apostle Paul specifically says that "... we do not want to be unclothed but to be clothed, so that what is mortal will be swallowed up by life" (II Cor. 5:4). Certainly, the passage contains some difficulties, but it is hard to escape the conclusion that Paul looks beyond the intermediate state of the disembodied soul to the resurrection body. To be "absent from the body" is to be "present with the Lord" (II Cor. 5:6), but if a deeper and more perfect fellowship with God is not made possible by the resurrection, what is the purpose of that great event?

The Testimony of Creation

One of the more pertinent interchanges between Robe and Erskine deals with the interpretation of that *textus classicus* for natural theology, Romans 1:18-23. However, even this passage fails to resolve crucial issues. In his *Review* James Fisher asserts, "Our Senses and Imagination, cannot assist us at all, in thinking upon the Divine Nature and Perfections" (Fisher 1743, 13, body). Robe's *Second Letter* to Fisher objects that this statement stands in direct contradiction to Romans 1:20. He continues:

> ... (tho' there can be no Representation formed on the Imagination of the Eternity, Omnipresence, Omniscience, and Omnipotence of God) yet our Senses and Imagination are greatly helpful to bring us to the Knowledge of the Divine nature and Perfections... (cited in Robe 1743, 59).

Erskine's response is twofold. First, he concedes an important point which Robe later uses.

> No doubt, *the Heavens declare the Glory of God*, and shew that a powerful God was the Maker of them; and the Apostle there says the same upon the Matter, that the visible *Frame* declares it hath an invisible *Framer*, and so the Light of Nature and Works of Creation teach the *Quod sit*, or *that God is*, and that he must be cloathed with such Perfections of Wisdom and Power as these Works declare: But if Mr. *Robe* think, that these visible things that strike our Senses and Imagination can lead us to the *Quid sit*, or *what God is*, and let us into the Knowledge or right Notion of the invisible divine Nature and Perfections,

then there would be little need of any other Bible than the visible Heavens (Erskine 1743, 53-54).

Robe's observation upon this distinction is that the wisdom and power of God, which are included in the *Quod sit*, are actually two of God's invisible perfections and therefore belong properly to the *Quid sit*. He further suggests that the light of nature is also sufficient to "... discover in some Measure to us [many other divine perfections];—such as his Eternity, Goodness, Immutability, Omniscience, &c..." (Robe 1743, 60-61). He specifically denies what Erskine implies he must hold, that is, that the saving knowledge of God is available aside from the effectual calling of the Holy Spirit.

Erskine's second thrust in his interpretation of Romans One is designed to cover for the concession which he has just made:

> The Design and Scope of the Apostle, in that Verse cited by Mr. *Robe*, is not so much to shew what Knowledge of God's Nature and Perfections Men may attain by the Visible Works of Creation, as rather, what Knowledge of him, attainable this Way, they smother and imprison, by *holding the Truth in Unrighteousness*, Ver. 18. and how all the Knowledge of God they had by the Creature, made them Err concerning the Creator, unto vain Imaginations about him, *Ver.* 21... (Erskine 1743, 55).

In other words, the knowledge of God available through creation leads men only to idolatry, and so does the knowledge of Christ afforded by an imaginary idea.

Erskine's observation that natural revelation does not profit the unsaved man is nothing new. John Calvin writes:

> As a consequence, men cannot open their eyes without being compelled to see him. Indeed, his essence is incomprehensible; hence, his divineness far escapes all human perception. But upon his individual works he has engraved unmistakable marks of his glory, so clear and so prominent that even unlettered and stupid folk cannot plead the excuse of ignorance (*Institutes* 1.5.1).

On the other hand, after a discussion of the corruption and idolatrous tendencies of the human heart, Calvin concludes:

> It is therefore in vain that so many burning lamps shine for us in the workmanship of the universe to show forth the glory of its Author. Although they bathe us wholly in their radiance, yet they can of themselves in no way lead us into the right path (*Institutes* 1.5.14).

Though this be true, it is not sufficient to support Erskine's statement that "Here was all the Knowledge of God their Senses and Imagination, in the Contemplation of the Creature, helped them unto. . ." (Erskine 1743, 55-56). Natural revelation does not "help" men toward idolatry. Rather, idolatry arises from the corruption of the human heart in spite of natural revelation. The proper tendency of the creation is to reveal the creator. Therefore, when Robe uses his "*Quod sit... Quid sit*" against him, Erskine has no further recourse. All he really adds in *Faith No Fancy* (besides a great many words) is the flat assertion of his occasionalist theory:

> Though it be by the intervention of our senses and imagination that we know these visible things; yet doth it hence follow, that our senses and imagination are great helps and assistants to us in the knowledge of the invisible things of God, or his divine nature and perfections?... Sense and imagination may sometimes give occasion to a man that hath reason, and the exercise of it to exert his rational powers upon spiritual and invisible things; but they can give no help and assistance thereto.... The outward senses and imagination are indeed greatly helpful to the knowledge of visible and corporeal things: These only are within that sphere. But to make them greatly helpful to the knowledge of God, his nature and perfections, and of spiritual and invisible things, is to exalt sense to the throne of reason, to invert the order of nature, and make... the bodily eye helpful to see what only the rational soul or intellectual eye can help us to see; such as *the invisible things of God, his eternal power and Godhead*, Rom. 1. 20 (Erskine 1745, 232).

Thus, even this text, which seemed to hold a promise of deciding the issue, must be judged insufficient for that purpose. Both Erskine and Robe acknowledge that nature plays a part in man's knowledge of God, but neither occasionalism nor empiricism is proven by the Apostle's words. Perhaps the only other thing which may be added is that Erskine's interpretation is, to say the very least, not obvious. It may be true, but it is not explicitly stated by any of the biblical passages which he cites. However, the same observation may be made about almost any metaphysical or epistemological theory. The more specific it becomes, the more it attempts to deal with various intellectual challenges, the less support it has from the Scriptures. That is certainly true of the system proposed by Jonathan Edwards as well, but a comparison of Erskine and Edwards belongs to the next chapter.

CHAPTER 5
A FINAL CONFRONTATION

Television talk shows frequently bring together proponents of differing world views to debate before the public eye. Unfortunately, a face to face discussion between Jonathan Edwards and Ralph Erskine is not possible. Any attempt at a final confrontation must take place through the evidence of the printed page.

The preceding chapters of this dissertation have dealt with the subject of mental images in the context of religious experience. The three principle figures who have been examined acknowledge the imaging power of the human mind, but to different ends. Edwards states that "… we can't think of things spiritual and invisible, without some exercise of this faculty [of the imagination] …" (Edwards 1972, 236). He then suggests that vivid mental images, even of Christ, may be helpful at times to faith, especially in the more ignorant. Taking his cue from Edwards, but expressing himself in stronger terms, James Robe insists that imaginary ideas of Christ as man are necessary to faith. Under the heading, "an imaginary idea of Christ as man," Robe includes not only vivid mental images of the body of the Lord, but also a general notion or picture of an embodied person. It is this latter which is strictly necessary to faith in Christ as the God-man. Finally, Erskine laments that mental images of the human body of Christ obtrude themselves into his devotional contemplations, thus defiling the purity of his worship. To him, every such image is idolatrous.

The issues which separate these men of God may be summarized in three questions which provide an outline for the present chapter: Do people think by means of images? Are all images of God or Christ idolatrous? How may preachers legitimately use images to touch souls for God? This portion of the study deals particularly with the contrasts between Edwards and Erskine.

Images and Thought

Conflict

Both Edwards and Erskine face the question of the mind's relation to the world. One way of focusing attention on their differing answers is to ask whether people normally or necessarily think in terms of images. A convenient entry into the subject is provided by Edwards' discussion of the nature of thought in Miscellany 782 (Edwards [1955] 1972, 113-26). Since thinking by means of the ideas of objects is very difficult, most thought makes use of signs. Signs of things "… are either the ideas of the names by which we are wont to call them or the idea of some external sensible thing that some way belongs to the things—some sensible image or resemblance, or some sensible part, or some sensible effect, or sensible concomitant, or a few sensible circumstances" (Edwards [1955] 1972, 116). Such signs may represent either physical or mental objects. For instance, grass may be represented by the word "grass" or by a mental image of grass, and God by the word "God," or by a mental image of a rock symbolizing Him as the refuge and strength of believers.

In addition to thinking by means of signs, "There is that which is more properly called *apprehension*, wherein the mind has a direct *ideal view* or *contemplation* of the thing thought of" (Edwards [1955] 1972,119). Such an "ideal apprehension" pertains either to the understanding (in which case it is a form of speculation) or to the will-affections. An example of the first type of apprehension would be the judgment that heaven is more pleasant than hell. The second form of ideal apprehension includes such ideas as:

... delight or comfort, or pleasure of body and mind, pain, trouble, or misery; and all ideal apprehensions of desires and longings, esteem, acquiescence, hope, fear, contempt, choosing, refusing, assenting, rejecting, loving, hating, anger, and the idea of all the affections of the mind, and all their motions and exercises; and all ideal views of dignity or excellency of any kind; and also all ideas of terrible greatness, or awful majesty, meanness, or contemptibleness, value and importance (Edwards [1955] 1972, 119-120).

It is, in short, "sensible knowledge."

The sense of the heart may be divided into natural and gracious affections. Even natural affections are further subdivided by Edwards into affections dealing with natural objects (e.g. delight in the beauty of grass) and affections dealing with supernatural objects (e.g. fear of the wrath of God). It is only in the final category of gracious affections that Edwards locates truly saving knowledge. While unregenerate human nature is capable of receiving all forms of speculative knowledge and natural affections, a sense of the beauty and sweetness of divine things does not come "... by assisting natural principles, but by infusing something supernatural" (Edwards [1955] 1972, 124). Edwards' analysis may be summarized in outline form as follows (most examples are supplied by the author, not Edwards).

1. Speculative Knowledge
    a)   Sign-Thoughts
        i)   Of Physical Objects
            (a) By Words—"grass"
            (b) By Mental Images—mental image of grass
        ii) Of Mental Objects
            (a) By Words—"God"
            (b) By Mental Images—mental image of rock symbolizing God
    b)   Ideal Apprehension of Things Pertaining to the Understanding—judgment that heaven is more pleasant than hell

2. Sensible Knowledge
   a) Natural Affections
      i) Of Natural Objects—delight in the beauty of grass
      ii) Of Spiritual Objects—fear of the wrath of God
   b) Gracious Affections—love for the beauty of Christ

Notice that Edwards separates words and mental images from ideal apprehensions, and that all forms of natural understanding are distinguished from gracious affections. The obvious question which needs to be asked regarding this scheme is, how do the various kinds of knowledge relate to each other?

Edwards specifically addresses the problem of relating speculative ideal apprehensions and natural affections to the believer's new sense of divine things. He writes:

> For as the spiritual excellency of the things of religion itself does depend on and presuppose those things that are natural in religion, they being, as it were, the substratum of this spiritual excellency, so a sense or ideal apprehension of the one depends in some measure on the ideal apprehension of the other (Edwards [1955] 1972, 125).

Although the new sense is very different from any species of natural knowledge, there exists a definite connection between the two. According to Edwards, natural and spiritual experiences are joined by two principles, "excellent congruity" and "a divine contrivance" (Edwards [1955] 1972, 126). The soul becomes convinced that the need of salvation, which is evident on natural principles, is fully satisfied by the way of salvation presented in the Gospel. The "... perfect suitableness there is... convinces 'em of the divine wisdom (that is beyond the wisdom of men) that contrived it" (Edwards [1955] 1972, 126). As indicated earlier in the dissertation, the same two principles seem to join vivid mental images of Christ and a relish for His beauty, at least on some occasions. The beauty of a mental image may become almost a type of the beauty of the Lord.

When Edwards' analysis of human knowledge is compared with that of Ralph Erskine, several similarities and some even more striking contrasts appear. Erskine's productions during the revival controversy do not discuss the nature of language or the possibility that images and words might both be signs of objects. In addition, his terminology varies from Edwards'. However, his separation of the faculties raises again the problem of relating different kinds of knowledge to each other. According to Erskine, "*Sense*, whether external or internal, ... hath for its object things corporeal; *reason*, properly things intellectual; and *faith*, things spiritual and supernatural...." The boundaries between these are absolute. "Sense cannot aspire to the sphere of reason, nor reason to the sphere of faith; and far less can sense and imaginary ideas do so" (Erskine 1745, 10). For Erskine, the connection between different kinds of knowledge rests in the sovereign appointment of God. God frequently makes events in the natural world to be occasions for evoking and improving innate knowledge. Innate knowledge is of two kinds—that given at physical birth and that imparted at spiritual birth. In both cases mental images, which belong to the realm of sense, have no inherent connection with true knowledge. In fact, they are a positive hindrance to true spiritual apprehension.

This conclusion stands in stark contrast to Edwards' supposition that mental images may serve a useful purpose in spiritual matters. If both thinkers recognize the difference between imagery and faith, and if both recognize that the decree of God connects experiences in the world with faith, why do they come to opposite conclusions regarding the possible value of mental images? In order to analyze this difference, it is helpful to recall the problems faced by Cartesianism.

The Cartesians concluded that the existence of thought implies a thinking substance. However, the supposition of a mental substance was found to lead to insuperable obstacles. How could the mind have a true knowledge of substances which were unlike itself? One natural alternative was to suggest that thought may be a function of matter and that the existence of separate minds is an unnecessary hypothesis. Such considerations posed the threat of materialism and offered a footing for atheism, and Christian philosophers felt their apologetic responsibilities heavily. Edwards' idealism involved an unusual response to this problem. Wallace Anderson summarizes his solution with a succinct contrast: "Berkeley's remedy for materialism was to argue that matter does not exist; Edwards' first and major step, on the other hand, was to argue that matter is not a substance" (Edwards 1980, 63). It is the infinite power of God, not the existence of some unidentifiable substance, which accounts for the resistance and solidity of bodies. God maintains their existence from moment to moment; they do not subsist by themselves (Edwards 1980, 65, 215). Therefore, as seen in chapter three of this study, the notion of causality is replaced by the sovereign operation of God. His power alone connects the events which are normally considered to be causal sequences.

Because Edwards eliminates substance as a property of created beings, his system does not have to contend with problems from the likeness principles. Since both spirits and matter have the same ontological status as ideas in the mind of God, human beings can receive true information through the senses. Ideas in our minds bear a genuine resemblance to the objects which they represent, for God who cannot lie connects our sense experiences with the external world. Interaction between mind and matter is no longer an insuperable obstacle because the barriers posed by postulating different substances have been broken down. Therefore, Edwards is able to consider the mind's use of signs, including mental images, as a genuine category of thought. In addition, remember that for Edwards conversion involves a change in the soul's habit or disposition, rather than in its nature. Because of this, natural knowledge (again including mental images) may be related to spiritual knowledge. The two species of consciousness are not kept in separate, airtight compartments.

Erskine, as opposed to Edwards, denies that the mind uses images or impressions from outside itself in order to think. Nothing from the external world can actually enter the intellect. Sense impressions only furnish occasions for the intellect to perform its proper work, and at times it can do this even apart from interaction with the body. For Erskine, the world appears to have a semi-independent status. Certainly, it is governed and sustained by the sovereign hand of God, but there are substances which exist as distinct from the being and substance of God. Therefore, unlike Edwards, Erskine does experience difficulty from the likeness principles. Images in the mind are related only to the world of sense. They cannot have any direct bearing on the workings of reason or on the birth and development of faith. Even animals are capable of mental imagery, for a dog distinguishes its master among a crowd of strangers. Since animals cannot reason, mental images do not possess the characteristics of true thought (Erskine 1745, 68-69). When God causes images in the mind to be occasions of reason or faith, He is making a connection which goes against the nature of the two events involved. In that sense Erskine's theory, like Malebranche's, includes the regular intervention of God's power in a way which is little short of miraculous. Edwards' system does not labor under such a necessity. For Edwards, the exercise of God's power does not come from outside the system to unite unlike substances. The differences between mind and matter are real enough, but the two are not unlike in essence, for God is the only true substance.

Resolution

Do people think by means of images? In spite of cavils by modern philosophers with obvious axes to grind, it is undoubtedly true that some people experience vivid mental images. In addition, it can be argued that mental imagery forms the basis for several kinds of rather ordinary experiences (Hannay 1971). The eighteenth-century theologians with whom this study is concerned all agree on the genuineness of the phenomenon. Therefore, the question is not whether mental imagery exists, but whether images constitute a valid aspect of thought, specifically of religious thought. Edwards' answer is that they do. His position commends itself for several reasons.

The first reason for receiving imagery as a significant aspect of thought is found in the symbolic nature of language. Edwards shows an awareness of this when he says that words may be signs of ideas. Think for a moment of the various types of words used in common speech. Some of them are terms of relation, such as "which" or "like." Others are emotive; that is, they signify what Edwards calls a sense of the heart. A third category may be designated picture words. All terms for physical objects and their movements fall into this category. It is not necessary that every use of the word "chair" should evoke a clear mental picture. But when "chair" occurs in the course of a story, the mind naturally runs through its catalog of past experience to identify in general the type of seating apparatus which seems most appropriate. Is it a self-righteous chair sitting primly in the corner and covered with Victorian brocade, or does it lounge beside a reading lamp waiting to enfold its guest in sensuous familiarity. The images which pass fleetingly before the mind's eye in such an exercise of the imagination may not attain to vividness and clearness, but their existence seems almost indisputable. In the example just considered, "chair" does not stand for a single mental image, but for a whole category of pictures.

When language passes from concrete objects to abstractions, the facile suggestion might be made that pictures have lost their usefulness. Erskine's theory involves the assumption that reason can do its work without relying on the senses, but careful consideration makes it clear that language (if not thought) is frequently bound to the world of sense. Scripture teaches that God is infinite, but is it possible to consider infinity without at least briefly imagining a vast expanse of something or of "nothingness?" It may be difficult to determine the extent to which the mind can think without language; however, language is involved in a large part of the mind's activity, and language itself commonly carries pictorial baggage.

A second reason for suggesting that images form a regular and acceptable part of the thinking process comes from Scripture. The Bible is not written in the antiseptic, precise language of science. God's message comes covered with the dust acquired by travel among commoners. The parables of Jesus are invitations to imagery, and much of the power of biblical prophecy lies in its vivid symbolism. Who, for instance, could forget the blood drinking whore, Babylon the Great. On a more positive note, consider the adornment of the tabernacle and the temple. Although God Himself is not represented by an image, the mind is certainly drawn to contemplate His glory by the sheer beauty and magnificence of His house. The temple is both a justification of religious art, and a suggestion that such art is not irrelevant. But would it not be irrelevant if images simply lay in the mind unconnected to the essential business of the soul? If the mind is not able to derive spiritual profit from meditation on biblical imagery, why is so much of God's revelation given in that form?

A final reason for recognizing the validity of mental imagery rests on the problems raised, by a denial of this concept. As noted at the end of the preceding chapter, Erskine's position tends to obscure three important biblical doctrines. His responses to Robe seem to imply: (1) minimizing the value of the incarnation, (2) denigrating the human body, and (3) rejecting the full scope of natural revelation. Certainly, Erskine intends to be orthodox, and his doctrine apart from the controversy over images is above reproach. However, it appears that he has been betrayed by his philosophy and by the heat of battle into committing several theological indiscretions.

Another problem with Erskine's position relates to his charge of mental idolatry. If Edwards and Robe are correct, and it is natural to think with images, then to call every mental image of Christ an idol means that God is at fault in His constitution of the human mind. On the other hand, if we do not think by means of images, if they lie in the mind essentially unrelated to reason or faith, then any kind of idolatry should be impossible. Obviously, Erskine does not draw such a conclusion, but if imaginary ideas of Christ are restricted to the sensitive faculty and cannot penetrate to the thinking soul, how can the soul actually contemplate them or worship by means of them? This poses an interesting dilemma. Either Erskine's psychology is incorrect, or his charge of mental idolatry is totally unfounded. The following pages will argue that the latter is at least partly justified. Therefore, his psychology becomes even more suspect.

Images and Idols

In chapters three and four of this study it has been suggested that the position of Edwards and Robe on mental images of Christ is less characteristic of Puritanism than that of Ralph Erskine. In order to substantiate that claim further it is helpful to review some typical expositions of the second commandment. Since Puritan opinion on the subject is frequently identical with that of Thomas Boston or John Calvin, these sources are cited indiscriminately in the following pages. The author believes that the insights of these godly men are generally true to the Scripture and should be given greater consideration by modern evangelicals.

Exegesis

Several Biblical passages are regularly cited as the basis of Puritan opposition to images of God. The first, of course, is the second commandment found in Exodus 20:4-6:

> You shall not make for yourself an idol, or any likeness of what is in heaven above or on the earth beneath or in the water under the earth. You shall not worship them or serve them; for I, the LORD your God, am a jealous God, visiting the iniquity of the fathers on the children, on the third and the fourth generations of those who hate Me, but showing lovingkindness to thousands, to those who love Me and keep My commandments.

Uniform Puritan exegesis insists that the first commandment, "You shall have no other gods before Me" (Exodus 20:3) fixes the object of worship as Jehovah, while the second establishes the proper means of worship. Consequently, the prohibition of idols applies both to images of other gods and to images of the true God. Such an elucidation of the commandments stands in stark contrast to that adopted by the Papists who combine the first and second commandments and thus "… sacrilegiously blot out the second commandment out of their catechises, dividing the tenth commandment into two…" (Watson 1806, 388). However, the repetition of the imperative is not sufficient to warrant a division of Exodus 20:17; the same criterion also marks off verses 3 and 4, and would divide the

Sabbath commandment in two—a method which yields the impossible total of twelve. In addition, the parallel passage, Deuteronomy 5:21, inverts the order of Exodus 20:17 so that the neighbor's wife is put before his house. If these represent separate commandments, "... what is ninth in the one would be tenth in the other, and contrarily, and so the order of these ten words... would be confounded" (Durham 1802, 395). Finally, the Reformed enumeration of the commandments is that adopted by the ancient Jews (Durham 1802, 66). Therefore, Exodus 20:3-6 represents two commandments which must be distinguished, not one. If they are two, the distinction must be between the proper object of worship and the proper manner of worship.

Confirmation of the preceding interpretation is found in Moses' exposition of the second commandment found in the fourth chapter of Deuteronomy. The chapter opens with a general injunction to heed the law which was given to Israel at Mount Sinai. On that occasion, Moses notes, the people saw no form of God (v. 12). This statement leads naturally into a reminder that they are neither to represent God by an image of any created thing nor to worship any of the natural manifestations of God's glory seen in the heavens (vv. 15-19). The crucial verses read as follows:

> So watch yourselves carefully, since you did not see any form on the day the LORD spoke to you at Horeb from the midst of the fire, so that you do not act corruptly and make a graven image for yourselves in the form of any figure, the likeness of male or female, (Deuteronomy 4:15-16).

As Calvin realized, these verses demonstrate conclusively that the pure worship of God must be imageless (Institutes 1.11.2). It is not simply heathen images that are prohibited; no image at all may be used in the worship of God.

Two other passages may be mentioned for their confirmation of the fact that images of the true God are prohibited. Romans 1:21-22 teaches that although men knew God,

> ... they turned the glory of that incorruptible God into the similitude of beasts and men, corruptible creatures. Their fault is not that they accounted these representations or images which they made, gods; but that they declined in their worship, in the worshipping of the true God by such images (Durham 1802, 72).

Another passage which is frequently noticed is Exodus 32, the account of Israel's worship of the golden calf. The calf image is not a representation of a heathen god, for the people held a feast to the LORD [Yahweh] and brought their offerings before the calf (vv. 5,8). Therefore, "... the image they set up was not itself acknowledged to be God, but as something to represent the true God" (Durham 1802, 74). Examples of Puritan exegesis related to the second commandment could easily be multiplied. However, it is also important to understand the reasons behind the prohibition of images of God.

Explanations

Expositions of the Shorter Catechism naturally focus their explanation of the second commandment on the reasons listed in the answer to question fifty-two: "The reasons annexed to the second commandment are, God's sovereignty over us, his propriety in us, and the zeal he hath to his own worship." When God calls Himself the Lord, He indicates that He has the sovereign right to tell us how to worship. God reinforces this right by the phrase "thy God"; we are His and must do as He says. If we do not, His jealousy is aroused; impure and idolatrous worship is like the adultery of an unfaithful wife, and God will not tolerate it (Boston [1853] 1980, 156-57; Vincent n.d., 166-67).

Another approach to the second commandment is to
examine ways in which images offer a challenge to specific
attributes of God. Images of God implicitly deny that He is
infinite Spirit. As Spirit, He has no body. Therefore, no true
picture of His divine nature can be made. "It is impossible to
make a picture of the soul, or to paint the angels, because they
are of a spiritual nature; much less then can we paint God by an
image, who is an infinite, uncreated Spirit." In addition, "Is it
not an absurd thing to bow down to the king's picture, when the
king himself is present? so to bow down to an image of God,
when God himself is every-where present" (Watson 1806, 387).

Obscuring God's spirituality by an image leads directly into
a related problem.

> When by our worship we tie the presence of the true God,
> to some place, image, statue, or relic, as if they had
> something in them, or communicated to them more
> divine [sic] than any other thing; or, as if God heard our
> prayers better at images, and by them; or, as if there were
> a more special presence of God there, or a more special
> dispensation of grace granted by them; as heathens
> supposed their gods dwelt visibly in their images, and did
> answer them there (Durham 1802, 79).

Thus, the tendency to develop sacred associations for favorite
images begins to place restrictions on God's sovereignty as well.
As Calvin notes, "For just as soon as a visible form has been
fashioned for God, his power is also bound to it. Men are so
stupid that they fasten God wherever they fashion him; and
hence they cannot but adore" (*Institutes* 1.11.9). When a picture
of God is placed in a church or a place of private devotion, the
thoughts of worshipers are almost inevitably attracted to it.
Once custom has established a connection between pious
sentiments and the picture, it is easy to feel (even if at first this
is denied) that prayers are more effective or more fervent in the
presence of that visible aid to worship. Thus, the sovereign God

becomes tied to a product of human hands, and His freedom to work where and when He will is obscured. Extreme examples of this tendency are not difficult to find even in Christendom. Witness the miracles which are supposed to take place at various Roman shrines around the world.

Because images cannot adequately picture the invisible God, but rather bind Him to a product of human hands, they subvert the full manifestation of His glory. As it is written by the prophet: "'To whom then will you liken Me that I would be his equal?' says the Holy One" (Isaiah 40:25). "I am the LORD, that is My name; I will not give My glory to another, nor My praise to graven images" (Isaiah 42:8). The realization of this truth looms larger than any other criticism in Calvin's extended denunciation of images (Institutes 1.11-12). Images, says Vincent, tend "... to lessen God in our esteem, who being the living God, and superlatively excellent, and infinitely removed above all his creatures, cannot, without great reflection of dishonour upon him, be represented by a dead image" (n.d., 161-62).

Images not only obscure the spirituality, sovereignty and glory of God. They also minimize the value of His Word. God "... discovered himself, Deut. iv. 15. 16. &c. by no likeness, but only by his word...," writes Durham (1802, 67). The papists, following Gregory the Great, have excused images as books of the uneducated, but "the stock is a doctrine of vanities" (Jeremiah 10:8, KJV). Habakkuk calls the molten image "a teacher of falsehood" (Habakkuk 2:18). Therefore, images of God only increase the ignorance of Him (Calvin, *Institutes* 1.11.5). It is through the teaching of the Word, and through that alone, that the uneducated can learn the mysteries of the Gospel. Because the Roman Church has failed in this sacred obligation, it has defrauded those under its care. "Indeed, those in authority in the church turned over to idols the office of teaching for no other reason than that they themselves were mute" (Calvin, *Institutes* 1.11.7).

Objections

Calvin and his spiritual descendants are by no means unaware of the arguments brought against their position. These may be listed under four separate headings: (1) Images are only symbols of God, not idols to be worshiped. (2) Images do not receive worship directly, but rather worship passes through them to God. (3) Honor paid to images is not the worship properly reserved for God alone. (4) Images were forbidden in the Old Testament, but they are now acceptable since God has become a man. These objections are examined below.

The first two objections to the Puritan position on images are related and may be discussed together. It is often urged that pictures of loved ones or of prominent figures are placed in private homes and in public buildings in order to honor them and to keep them in remembrance. These pictures are never confused for the persons they represent, nor do they arouse jealousy. Generally, people are flattered to have their likenesses displayed. In the same way, images of God are erected in order to honor Him and to keep the mind occupied with spiritual things. The standard answer to this excuse is to note that frequently the heathen think of their images as mere symbols of deity. As Calvin says:

> Read the excuses that Augustine refers to as having been pretended by the idolaters of his own age: when they were accused, the vulgar sort replied that they were not worshiping that visible object but a presence that dwelt there invisibly. Those who were of what he called "purer religion" stated that they were worshiping neither the likeness nor the spirit; but that through the physical image they gazed upon the sign of the thing that they ought to worship (*Institutes* 1.11.9).

The heathen make many images of each of their gods, thus demonstrating that an image is not identical to the deity. Worship in the presence of an image does not normally terminate in that image as if it could do something by itself. It passes on to the god which is represented. Even the Jews who fell down before the golden calf did not think it was God. They merely worshiped Jehovah through it (Boston [1853] 1980, 152). Therefore, images which symbolize the true God, and which may become a focal point for worship, are precisely the kind of thing condemned by the second commandment.

Although men may say images are only symbols, it is perfectly clear that great reverence is paid to them in the Roman and Greek Churches. Therefore, a linguistic distinction has been drawn between the service given to an image (*dulia*) and the worship reserved for God alone(*latria*). Two refutations of this piffling distinction may be offered. Calvin notes that the emphasis placed on images destroys any supposed difference between *dulia* and true worship. The ridiculous assertions of delegates to the Council of Nicea (787) help to clarify the issue.

> Theodosius, Bishop of Amorium, pronounces anathema against all who are unwilling that images be adored. Another imputes all the misfortunes of Greece and the East to the crime that images had not been adored.... Indeed, John, the legate of the Easterns, moved by even greater heat, warned that it would be better to admit all brothels into the city than to deny the worship of images. Finally, it was determined by the consent of all that the Samaritans are worse than all heretics, yet image fighters are worse than the Samaritans. Besides, lest the play should go unapplauded, a clause is added: let those who, having an image of Christ, offer sacrifice to it rejoice and exult. Where now is the distinction between latria and dulia, by which they are wont to hoodwink God and men? For the Council accords, without exception, as much to images as to the living God (Calvin, *Institutes* 1.11.116).

Scripture provides a second refutation of the supposed difference between service given to images and the worship offered to God. As Calvin aptly demonstrates, that difference does not exist.

> Let us drop fine distinctions and examine the thing itself. When Paul reminds the Galatians what they were like before they were illumined in the knowledge of God, he says that "they exhibited dulia toward beings that by nature were no gods" [Gal. 4:8 p.]. When he does not call it latria, is their superstition for this reason excusable? Assuredly, by labeling that perverse superstition dulia, he condemns it no less than if he had used the word "latria" (Institutes 1.12.3).

Furthermore, both angels and godly men of the Bible refuse to receive homage. Certainly, it is acceptable to bow to an earthly ruler and in this way give him civil honor, just as it is permissible when "… doing some civil business, as tying the shoe, or such like" (Durham 1802, 71). "But because any reverential act that has been joined with religion cannot but savor of something divine…," it is impossible to kneel before God's representative "… without detracting from God's glory" (Calvin, *Institutes* 1.12.3). The service, or *dulia*, which is considered proper for images is not less than that refused by an angel (Revelation 19:10; 22:8-9) or by Peter (Acts 10:25-26). Therefore, it stands condemned.

The final objection to the Puritan position on images relates more directly to the subject of this dissertation. It is that images which were forbidden in the Old Testament are now acceptable because of the incarnation. If images are rejected under the Law because God is invisible, surely now that the Lord has taken on a body, His human form may be pictured. As plausible as this argument seems, it is consistently rejected.

Because the point is so important, it bears some repetition:

Though Christ be a man, yet he is God too, and therefore no image can nor may represent him...; and if it should stir up devotion, that is worshipping by an image, which is idolatry here forbidden (Boston [1853] 1980, 151).

It is not lawful to have pictures of Jesus Christ, because his divine nature cannot be pictured at all, and because his body, as it is now glorified, cannot be pictured as it is; and because, if it do not stir up devotion, it is in vain; if it do stir up devotion, it is a worshipping by an image or picture, and so a palpable breach of the second commandment (Vincent n.d., 162).

Epiphanius seeing an image of Christ hanging in a church brake it in pieces, it is Christ's Godhead, united to his manhood, that makes him to be Christ: therefore, to picture his manhood, when we cannot picture his Godhead, is a sin, because we make him to be but half Christ, we separate what God hath joined, we leave out that which is the chief thing, which makes him to be Christ (Watson 1806, 389).

And if it be said man's soul cannot be painted, but his body may, and yet that picture representeth a man; I answer, it doth so, because he has but one nature, and what representeth that representeth the person; but it, is not so with Christ: his Godhead is not a distinct part of the human nature, as the soul of man is (which is necessarily supposed in every living man), but a distinct nature, only united with the manhood in that one person, Christ, who has no fellow; therefore what representeth him must not represent a man only, but must represent Christ, Immanuel, God-man, otherwise it is not his image. Beside, there is no warrant for representing him in his manhood; nor any colourable possibility of it, but as men fancy; and shall that be called Christ's portraiture? would that be called any other man's portraiture which were drawn at men's pleasure, without regard to the pattern? Again, there is no use of it; for either that image behoved to have but common estimation with other images, and that would wrong Christ, or a peculiar respect and reverence, and so it sinneth against this commandment that forbiddeth all religious reverence to images, but he being God and so the object of worship, we must either divide his natures, or say, that image or picture representeth not Christ (Durham 1802, 68).

It is noteworthy that Scripture condemns images "in the form of corruptible man" along with other kinds of images (Romans 1: 23), and that the Apostle makes no mention of a change in principle based on the incarnation. As a matter of fact, images would appear to be a gross form of the fleshly estimation of Christ rejected elsewhere by Paul (II Corinthians 5:16). Paul's attitude parallels the utter disregard for Christ's physical appearance which is evident in the Gospels and which continues on into the early church. Calvin notes that images in churches are rejected by the Council of Elvira in Spain (ca. A.D. 305), by Augustine, and in general during the first five hundred years of the Christian era (Institutes 1.11.6,9,13).

Thus, theological, Scriptural and historical considerations are presented by reformed authors as evidence that images of God are idolatrous and that pictures of Christ are included in the prohibition of images. James Robe and Jonathan Edwards appear to accept many of these principles, but they wish to make room for mental images of Christ as man. It remains to be asked whether their approach can be justified on the basis of Scripture or Puritan precedent. In order to do that it is necessary to see how the second commandment is applied to various kinds of images and then to inquire whether there are any legitimate exceptions.

Application

The primary principle governing Puritan application of the second commandment is that no representation of the Trinity or of any Person of the Godhead is allowed, whether by any natural or by any artificial object. The second commandment specifically forbids likenesses of anything in the heavens, on the earth, or in the water. The contents of the earth and water are obvious enough, but in addition to the birds, sun, moon and stars, Boston lists God, angels and the saints in heaven ([1853] 1980, 128). Calvin is probably correct in omitting the latter (*Institutes* 2.8.17). James Durham provides a list which is representative of the kinds of forbidden images mentioned by several authors.

> 1. We simply condemn any delineating of God, or the Godhead, or Trinity; such as some have upon their buildings, or books, like a sun shining with beams, and the Lord's name, Jehovah, in it or any other way....
>
> 2. All representing of the persons as distinct, as to set out the Father (personally considered) by the image of an old man, as if he were a creature, the Son under the image of a lamb or young man, the Holy Ghost under the image of a dove, all which wrongeth the Godhead exceedingly... (Durham 1802, 67).

Durham's list is given in almost the same words by Boston ([1853] 1980, 150), and elements of it appear in other works.

The references to the sun and to an image of a lamb raise the issue of metaphors. It might be thought that even if images in human shape are rejected, still pictures could be drawn, based on biblical metaphors, which would represent God in a more remotely symbolic fashion. Watson, however, suggests that the same principles apply in both cases:

> Though God is pleased to stoop to our weak capacities, and set himself out in scripture by eyes, to signify his omnisciency; and hands to signify his power; yet it is very absurd, from metaphors and figurative expressions, to bring an argument for images and pictures; for, by that rule, God may be pictured by the sun and the element of fire, and by a rock; for God is set forth by these metaphors in scripture; and sure the papists themselves would not like to have such images made of God (Watson 1806, 389).

After all, if the heathen use natural objects to symbolize their deities, how can Christians claim to be any different if they follow the same practices.

Even though God Himself may not be represented by any created thing, there is an occasional grudging admission that visible symbols may be used to convey spiritual truth. The cherubim found in the tabernacle and temple form an interesting case study. Calvin calls them "paltry little images" whose sole purpose is to show

> ... that images are not suited to represent God's mysteries. For they had been formed to this end, that veiling the mercy seat with their wings they might bar not only human eyes but all the senses from beholding God, and thus correct men's rashness (*Institutes* 1.11.3).

Owen insists that they are not images of angels since angels are spirits and do not really look like winged creatures. He calls them "... mere *hieroglyphicks*, to represent the constant tender love and watchfulness of God over the ark of his covenant..." (Erskine 1745, 332). Durham seems even more uncomfortable over the problem posed by the cherubim. He would like to ban images of angels altogether, but he hesitates to take too firm a stand:

> From this ground also it would seem, that painting of angels might be condemned, as a thing impossible, they being spirits which no corporeal thing can represent, beside that the representing of them has some hazard with it: and for those cherubims that were made by God's direction under the Old Testament, they were rather some emblem of the nature and service of angels, as being full of zeal, and always (as it were) upon wing ready to obey God's will, than any likeness of themselves (Durham 1802, 68-69).

Thus, Erskine is in good company when he casts a rather suspicious glance at Solomon's temple. After all, Aaron's calf was condemned by God, but in the temple twelve oxen upheld the molten sea (I Kings 7:23-25). These artistic productions are excused "… seeing all things there were done by the command of God, and the figures themselves were types of spiritual things, which were to have their accomplishment in Christ" (Erskine 1745, 155). The bronze serpent made by Moses is clearly a happier example. The worship of this "Nehushtan" by later generations demonstrates how easily even lawful images may be abused (Durham 1802, 69; Boston [1853] 1980, 151; Watson 1806, 388-89). It is significant, therefore, that both Edwards and Robe take a very positive approach to the visible and imaginable aspects of Old Testament types and symbols. This will receive further attention shortly.

Not only does the standard Puritan position reject any images of the Divine Being and look askance at visible symbols of spiritual truth, but it also clearly warns of the danger of mental idolatry. Since the imagination is the repository of images from the external world, it is chiefly responsible for man's propensity to create idols. The "vain imaginations" of the heathen are the source of images in the form of "corruptible man, and [of] birds and fourfooted beasts, and creeping things" (Romans 1:21, 23, KJV). As Calvin notes, man's mind, "… so to speak, is a perpetual factory of idols," so that "… it dares to imagine a god according to its own capacity; as it sluggishly plods, indeed is overwhelmed with the crassest ignorance, it conceives an unreality and an empty appearance as God" (*Institutes* 1.11.8). Vincent insists that idolatry occurs not only when people worship external images, but also "When they have in their worship carnal imaginations, and representations of God in their minds, as if he were an old man sitting in heaven, or the like" (Vincent n.d., 161). Watson includes "All ideas" as well as "… portraitures, shapes, images of [G]od…" in his list of sinful likenesses (Watson 1806, 386). According to Durham, "There should not be in us any carnal apprehensions

of God, as if he were like anything that we could imagine..."
(Durham 1802, 64). Finally, Thomas Boston rejects "Every
similitude whatsoever for religious use and service..., though it
be merely by the imagination, and not by the hand; for the
words are universal, *any likeness*" (Boston [1853] 1980, 150).
He elaborates this point as follows:

> Now, under this article of religious imagery is forbidden,
>
> 1*st*, The making any representation or image of God in
> our mind, all carnal imaginations of him, as to conceive of
> him like a reverend old man, &c. Acts xvii. 29. for God is
> the object of our understanding, not our imagination,
> being invisible. This is mental idolatry, which the best are
> in hazard of (Boston [1853] 1980, 150).

In these warnings concerning mental idolatry, two
principles are operative. First, the imagination is the root of all
idolatry because of its power freely to fashion images which are
not in accord with reality. Second, it is generally assumed that
the same kinds of external images which are forbidden are also
prohibited in the mind.

Exceptions

In the controversy over mental images, Robe finds himself
cast into a defensive position. His argument amounts to an
assertion that there are exceptions to the general rule. Can that
position be sustained? Perhaps it will be helpful to review
briefly the tradition which he faces. The basic premise is that all
visible representations of God are sinful. Second, images of
Christ are forbidden because His divine nature cannot be
pictured; a picture can only represent His human nature which
is but half a Christ. If it stirs up devotion, that is idolatrous
worship; if it does not, the picture serves no useful purpose.
Third, even mental images of God are specifically condemned.
In order to demonstrate the validity of some mental images of
Christ, these three premises must be weakened.

A modification of the first principle is suggested by the fact that symbolic representations of spiritual truth or of God's attributes are occasionally allowed by Puritan theology. Robe specifically defends mental images representing God and based on biblical types and metaphors. As noted earlier he says that the imagination helps the superior faculties to conceive of God by presenting to them images of sensible objects which are used as symbols of spiritual truth. The brazen serpent was a type of Christ which only became sinful when it was worshiped. In the same fashion the Israelites held an imaginary idea of the high priest in their minds when he went behind the veil on the day of atonement. In this way, they were led toward the apprehension of a deeper spiritual realization of Christ's office as mediator. He says that, "They behoved indeed, by the Exercise of their Imagination, when the Situation of the Types required it, to form an idea of the Type, that their Understanding and Judgment might be instructed in the Knowledge of the Anti-type..." (Robe 1743, 13). Robe complains that James Fisher wholly misunderstands the usefulness of types when he writes that "... the great design of all the types..." was to "... lead the people off from these figures that were the objects of their external senses..." (Fisher 1743, 6). If that is the case, says Robe, "... it had been better not to have instituted these Types..., being if they had not been instituted, they would have been in no danger from them..." (Robe 1743, 12).

Edwards' typology and his analysis of language both suggest the same perspective. In the preceding section, it has been suggested that sign-thought is a valid aspect of mental activity. Therefore, it seems reasonable to conclude that visible objects may serve the mind as signs for God in one or another of His perfections. Although such signs form no part of truly gracious affections, they may accompany them. Thus, an impression of outward brightness may accompany an affectionate taste of

God's glory. In that case, the brightness may be taken as a sign-thought of the glory of God. It need not represent the divine essence or any of the persons of the Godhead directly.

A more difficult problem arises when the mental image represents the Lord Jesus Christ. In accepting some such images, Robe and Edwards appear to be weakening the second premise of the Puritan position on images. The union of Christ's two natures in one person forms the primary basis for Puritan rejection of images of the Savior; to present the mind's eye with half a Christ is heresy at best, or idolatry at worst. Robe's clear response is that it is not heretical to think of the humanity of Christ apart from His deity. Therefore, it is permissible to have an imaginary idea of His human body. Such an idea does not preclude a simultaneous realization of His deity. In fact, an imaginary idea of Christ as man must be combined with an intellectual comprehension of his deity in order to arrive at a true and complete conception of the Mediator.

Robe's position implies conclusions which he might well have rejected. Erskine charges Robe with teaching that external images of Christ are also lawful (Erskine 1745, 155). The accusation is based on an inaccurate reading of one sentence in Robe's Fourth Letter (Robe 1743, 44). Nevertheless, the connection between mental and external images does seem to be very close. If meditation involving a mental image does not blasphemously divide the natures of Christ, why should meditation stimulated by a picture of the Lord be subject to that charge?

There is an approach to the problem, not used by either Robe or Edwards, which offers some promise. It is based on the recognition that pictures of historical events are permitted by God. Calvin appears to have pushed the door ajar for lawful images of Christ to enter (though it was certainly not shoved open by his Puritan successors). Consider the following:

> But because sculpture and painting are gifts of God, I seek
> a pure and legitimate use of each.... We believe it wrong
> that God should be represented by a visible appearance,
> because he himself has forbidden it [Ex. 20:4] and it
> cannot be done without some defacing of his glory....
> Therefore it remains that only those things are to be
> sculptured or painted which the eyes are capable of
> seeing;... Within this class some are histories and events,
> some are images and forms of bodies without any
> depicting of past events. The former have some use in
> teaching or admonition; as for the latter, I do not see what
> they can afford other than pleasure. And yet it is clear that
> almost all the images that until now have stood in
> churches were of this sort. From this, one may judge that
> these images had been called forth not out of judgment or
> selection but of foolish and thoughtless craving (*Institutes*
> 1.11.12).

It is not clear whether Calvin intends to allow for historical
pictures which include a likeness of the Savior. However, such
an interpretation seems at least plausible. At any rate, he does
suggest a valuable distinction between portraits and depictions
of Gospel history.

In order to see the significance of such a distinction,
consider the manner in which Jesus Christ revealed God (La
Shell 1976, 69-70). The Apostles did not recognize Him as the
Son of God because of His countenance but on the basis of His
words and deeds. The signs which Jesus performed were the
evidence to which the Apostle John pointed as proof of the
deity of Christ (John 20:30-31). Indeed, our Lord Himself said:

> Do you not believe that I am in the Father and the Father
> is in me? The words that I say to you I do not speak on my
> own authority, but the Father who dwells in me does his
> works. Believe me that I am in the Father and the Father
> is in me, or else believe on account of the works
> themselves (John 14:10-11).

Any attempt to depict the person of Christ by a portrait
must fail. His deity cannot be pictured at all, and His character

can only be suggested. What is often produced is the image of a divinized man, which Christ most certainly is not. However, visible representations of New Testament events may convey the message of the deity of Christ, not by portraying His person in a certain fashion, but by setting forth His divine works. Obviously, there is sometimes a fine line dividing the two kinds of art. Some paintings of historical events contain virtual portraits of Christ, so that the focus of attention is drawn to His countenance rather than to His activity. Nevertheless, the general distinction seems to be clear enough. In addition, it appears to accommodate the most important insights in the psychology of Edwards and Robe. Sign-thoughts may legitimately be used in two ways. The character of God in His various perfections may be represented by symbols, and events in the life of Christ on earth may be imaged in the mind's eye. The same criteria also seem applicable, within cautious limits, to external figures.

In spite of these concessions, not all of the imaginary ideas defended by Edwards and Robe can be justified. Reports of visions include pathetic images of a crucified Savior and beautiful images of a glorified Savior. In both cases the visions must be regarded as portraits rather than signs of historical events. For this reason, it is necessary for Robe and Edwards to defend mental images on the basis that they are involuntary. This constitutes a weakening of the third Puritan premise regarding religious images—that mental images of God are sinful.

Edwards appears to be saying that vivid mental images which arise spontaneously as a result of truly gracious affections may be beneficial (at least to the ignorant). Those which result from elevated but non-gracious affections are deceitful and harmful because they induce a false assurance of salvation. That is a step in the right direction because if images are inherent in man's thinking, it is only possible to locate the sin of idolatry in the attitude of the imaging subject. But more must be said. He who accepts his images as visions from heaven, he who trusts in them and rejoices in them—that man is an idolater. Notice that such an interpretation entails a paradox. The man who appears to benefit most from a mental image of Christ is the one who benefits least. He is the one who may actually be harmed by what he perceives. Thus, it seems impossible to allow Edwards' suggestion that imaginary ideas of Christ resemble Old Testament types. They are too dangerous for such a positive evaluation.

How then should involuntary mental portraits of Christ be treated by those who experience them? Erskine's comparison of mental idolatry with mental adultery suggests some important clues. A man cannot always avoid seeing a beautiful woman or being attracted to her. Mental adultery does not consist in physical sight, but in cultivating the mental image of that woman for the purpose of sexual stimulation. In the same way, it is possible to walk past a portrait of Christ in a museum without yielding to any temptation to meditate on God through its instrumentality. When a mental image comes into the mind without a deliberate volition, its content must be evaluated. If it is symbolic of God's attributes or if it represents an event in the life of the Lord Jesus, it may be entertained with caution. If it consists of a virtual portrait of the Savior, it ought to be rejected rather than fondled. These suggestions may not commend themselves to all students, but to the present author they seem to strike a scriptural balance between the important psychological insights of Jonathan Edwards and the equally important theological cautions of Ralph Erskine.

Images and Preaching

The eighteenth-century controversy over imaginary ideas of Christ arose out of a revival fostered by biblical preaching. During the awakening, opponents frequently charged revival preachers with deliberately stirring up the passions of their hearers. Elevated passions were considered by many to be the cause of unfortunate excesses of the period, including the visions reported by some converts. Therefore, preaching was a controversial subject in the mid-eighteenth century. There was no general agreement on the proper means of addressing men in the name of God. Puritan wisdom on the subject had begun to lose its hold on many preachers, but not on Jonathan Edwards.

The Puritan Ideal

The Puritan ideal for preachers is clearly delineated by William Perkins. His influence is formative on the early direction of Puritanism, and he remains representative of the movement even after it becomes mature. In *The Calling of the Ministerie*, Perkins insists that the minister ought to speak in the evidence and demonstration of the Spirit. From an examination of I Corinthians 14:24-25 he concludes:

> Now to speake in the demonstration of Gods Spirit, is to speake in such *plainenesse*, and yet such *powerfulnesse*, as that the capacities of the simplest, may perceiue, not man, but God teaching them in that plainenesse, and the conscience of the mightiest may feel, not man, but God-reproouing them in that powerfulnes (Perkins 1612-13, 2:430).

Plainness and power are not unrelated. In order for the common man to be moved by the Word of God, he must first understand it. Contrary to a common misconception the famous Puritan "plain style" does not include a rejection of all the arts of persuasion. It is a conscious reaction against the learned and ornate performances which were much admired by certain members of the more educated class. Greek and Latin phrases are avoided, as are stories from classical sources which might be unfamiliar to the masses. The authority of the message rests on the exposition of the Scripture rather than on citation of human testimony. Perkins' important treatise, *The Arte of Prophecying*, establishes the pattern for Puritan preachers for over a century. In it he sets forth:

> THE ORDER AND SVMME of the sacred and onely methode ^.
>
> 1. To read the text distinctly out of the Canonicall Scriptures.
>
> 2. To give the sense and vnderstanding of it being read, by the Scripture it selfe.
>
> 3. To collect a few and profitable points of doctrine out of the naturall sense.
>
> 4. To apply (if he have the gift) the doctrines rightly collected, to the life and manners of men, in a simple and plaine speech (Perkins, 2.673)

Exposition, doctrines and applications—this is precisely the pattern later to be recommended by the *Directory for the Public Worship of God* drawn up by the Westminster Assembly. That it is not simply an ideal but is actually practiced by Puritan preachers is adequately demonstrated by an examination of their sermons (Davies 1948, 191).

The Puritan ideal is subject to degeneration in a number of ways related to the three major aspects of preaching. The exposition of Scripture may be minimized by elevating private reason or personal revelations. The one is the method of the rationalist, the other of the enthusiast. The doctrinal aspect of preaching can serve as a focus for corruption either by promulgating heretical views or, more often, by preaching the truth in an arid intellectual fashion while despising the proper means of persuasion. Finally, the application can become the whole of the sermon resulting either in a lecture on morality or in an impassioned harangue. All of these distortions of the homiletical art are exemplified in seventeenth and eighteenth century preaching.

Fashionable preaching of the eighteenth century tends to carry heavy intellectual baggage on the assumption that men can only be brought to God through enlightening the understanding. Fear of enthusiasm runs high, for memories of sectarian excesses during Commonwealth days are still fresh. Locke's distinction between the will and the affections allows him the luxury of despising the emotions as an inferior faculty. Eloquence is suitable for speech which seeks merely to entertain, but it is wholly out of place in more serious discourse. The methods of rhetoric are "Arts of Fallacy" by which "... Men find pleasure to be Deceived" (Locke 1975, 508). He continues:

> ... all the Art of Rhetorick, besides Order and Clearness, all the artificial and figurative application of Words Eloquence hath invented, are for nothing else but to insinuate wrong *Ideas*, move the Passions, and thereby mislead the Judgment; and so indeed are a perfect cheat... (Locke 1975, 508).

Jonathan Edwards and the revival ministers in general run into opposition partly because they are attempting to restore evangelical fervor to the proclamation of the Gospel. Edwards deplores the trends of his day:

> I know it has long been fashionable to despise a very earnest and pathetical way of preaching; and they, and they only have been valued as preachers, that have shown the greatest extent of learning, and strength of reason, and correctness of method and language; but I humbly conceive it has been for want of understanding, or duly considering human nature. . . (Edwards 1972, 387).

The proper method of preaching, on the other hand, is a suitable combination of doctrinal truth and affectionate application and delivery:

I think an exceeding affectionate way of preaching about the great things of religion, has in itself no tendency to beget false apprehensions of them; but on the contrary a much greater tendency to beget true apprehensions of them, than a moderate, dull, indifferent way of speaking of 'em. An appearance of affection and earnestness in the manner of delivery, if it be very great indeed, yet if it be agreeable to the nature of the subject, and ben't beyond a proportion to its importance and worthiness of affection, and there be no appearance of its being feigned or forced, has so much the greater tendency to beget true ideas or apprehensions in the minds of the hearers, of the subject spoken of, and so to enlighten the understanding: and that for this reason, that such a way or manner of speaking of these things does in fact more truly represent them, than a more cold and indifferent way of speaking of them (Edwards 1972, 386-87).

What Edwards is, in essence, recommending is a return to the original balance of the Puritan ideal. The exposition of Scripture and the doctrines contained in it must be balanced by effective application to the heart. It is in this matter of application that Edwards makes his most significant contribution to the art of preaching.

Affectionate Application

A number of techniques for pressing home the claims of Christ are generally recognized and approved by evangelical ministers of the sixteenth through eighteenth centuries. They include: the repetition of important ideas, direct and personal address to the hearers, illustration of difficult points by stories or analogies, a fervent manner of speaking, and application of the message to the particular needs of the congregation. All of these may be seen to some extent in William Perkins, and to a greater or lesser degree they continue to be used by those who are concerned to preach for spiritual results. Whitefield's fervency is so well known that perhaps a reminder is needed that other evangelicals were also eager for souls. This excerpt from the anti-revivalist, Ralph Erskine, is quite typical of his sermons:

> Is Satan desiring to have you? Alas! sirs, let this put you in mind that Christ is desiring to have you. Satan is desiring to have you, that he may destroy you; but Christ is desiring to have you, that he may save you. There are two suitors, then, about you this day, that have a great desire after you. O sirs, tell me, which of them shall have you? Which of them will you yield unto? A praying devil, or a praying Jesus? The devil is praying to God that he may have you; and praying you to come to him, and serve him, as the god of this world, and offering you all worldly advantages. Christ is praying to God that he may have you; and praying you to come to him, and sending us to pray you in his stead, that you may be reconciled to God. O! come, come to Jesus; and plead upon his prayer and intercession. Then surely your desire, and not Satan's, shall prevail; for Christ's desire is heard of God. O! shall not his desire be heard of you? If you neglect Christ this day, you give way to the devil's getting his desire about you. Therefore, O! come, come; come to Jesus, and you are safe, though Satan should exert his utmost to obtain you (Erskine 1865, 452-3).

Edwards, then, is not unique in stressing the need for an affectionate mode of address to sinners. His contribution lies in his use of vivid images. In his most powerful sermons Edwards employs a style of preaching which may be designated as sensory. He does not simply use illustrations to make the truth clear, a thoroughly respectable and approved practice. He even does more than visualize the truth, for his hearers are not merely made observers of a drama. Rather, they are caught up into the sermon and made participants in the action. His purpose is to enable the soul to savor the truth, to experience it in the act of listening. The more that the senses are enlisted in the cause of truth, the more effective will be the preacher's presentation of it.

The differences between the types of preaching already discussed may be illustrated by considering alternate approaches to the subject of hell. An intellectual preacher might provide a series of carefully constructed arguments proving the existence and nature of a place of eternal damnation. An affectionate preacher such as Erskine would add to this an urgent appeal for his hearers to flee the terrors of hell and seek refuge in the arms of Jesus. Beyond these two Edwards seeks in such a sermon to ". . . impart the sensible idea in all immediacy; in the new psychology, it must become, not a traveler's report nor an astrologer's prediction, but an actual descent into hell" (Miller [1949] 1973, 146). When men virtually begin to feel the fires of the pit, it is no wonder that they cry out in terror. Best known is Edwards' Enfield sermon in which he suspends his audience over the gaping pit of hell supported by a mere spider's thread (Edwards [1834] 1974, 2:7-12). Similar examples are not difficult to find. Consider "The End of the Wicked Contemplated by the Righteous." Taking his text from Revelation, 18:20 he stresses the joy of the righteous at the condemnation of the wicked. In the application, Edwards addresses those who have not yet come to Christ. He tells them that the godly ministers who warned them and even their own parents and friends will rejoice in their destruction.

> And when you shall stand before the tribunal at the left hand, among devils, trembling and astonished, and shall have the dreadful sentence passed upon you, you will at the same time see the blessed company of saints and angels at the right hand rejoicing, and shall hear them shout forth the praises of God, while they hear your sentence pronounced....
>
> Perhaps there are now some godly people, to whom you are near and dear, who are tenderly concerned for you, are ready to pity you under all calamities, and willing to help you; and particularly are tenderly concerned for your poor soul, and have put up many fervent prayers for

you. How will you bear to hear these singing for joy of heart, while you are crying for sorrow of heart, and howling for vexation of spirit, and even singing the more joyful for the glorious justice of God which they behold in your eternal condemnation (Edwards [1834] 1974, 210).

It is important to understand clearly the philosophical justification for such an approach. Perry Miller has badly overstated the case, for he represents Edwards as a manipulative behavioral psychologist who "... deliberately committed himself to administering the kind of shock that would transform the recipient, by psychological processes, into the kind of person who would absorb the shock in only one way" (Miller [1949] 1973, 158). What Miller neglects to consider is that Edwards distinguishes the Christian's new sense of divine things from anything that is within the capacity of the natural man. Edwards uses Lockean terminology to describe how a new simple idea of the sweetness of Christ is supernatually impressed on the mind of man, but the believer's new sense is not given by the words of any preacher, no matter how eloquent. It comes directly from God. Of what use, then, is preaching? Edwards' use of vivid images in his preaching raises a number of significant problems.

Crucial Questions

What is the relationship between preaching and the touch of God upon the soul? This issue may be broken down into four separate questions. First, what is the rationale for preaching? Second, why does Edwards attempt to impress his hearers with such vivid images of salvation and damnation? Third, how is vivid preaching related to images in the mind of the hearer? Fourth, what kinds of images should a preacher attempt to paint?

First Question: The Rationale for Preaching

Edwards explains that the rationale for preaching is derived from God's decree. Just as God has ordained the physical world as a collection of types of spiritual truths, so He has ordained preaching as his means of bringing spiritual light into the soul.

> And the impressing divine things on the hearts and affections of men, is evidently one great and main end for which God has ordained, that his Word delivered in the Holy Scriptures, should be opened, applied, and set home upon men in preaching.... God hath appointed a particular and lively application of his Word, to men, in the preaching of it, as a fit means to affect sinners, with the importance of the things of religion, and their own misery, and necessity of a remedy, and the glory and sufficiency of a remedy provided; and to stir up the pure minds of the saints, and quicken their affections, by often bringing the great things of religion to their remembrance, and setting them before them in their proper colors... (Edwards 1959, 115-16).

Second Question: Why Use Vivid Images

It may be asked why God has established vivid, or even sensory preaching as His means of affecting men. The answer seems to lie in understanding the parallels between nature and grace. In the natural realm, the five senses are the source of a man's simple ideas. In the spiritual realm, a new sense is the source of the believer's simple ideas of divine things. The external means by which God moves men are found in the natural realm, while all of the actual work of the Spirit is supernatural. God has ordained that effective preaching should appeal to the natural senses because this parallels his work in the realm of grace. In other words, He uses most those means which are most suited to the ends He desires to accomplish. Since true religion consists, in large measure, in godly affections and since the affections are raised by some new light in the understanding (Edwards 1972, 386; Edwards 1959, 266), it is appropriate that the understanding be approached in the most effective way, that is, through sensible images impressed by affectionate preaching.

Edwards does not summarize his theory of preaching in precisely this way. However, it is in some such manner that one must account for his preaching style, his defense of his method as God ordained, his empirical psychology, and his emphasis on the new sense of the regenerate. Edwards' typology suggests the concept of parallelism between God's work and the preacher's, and this seems to be the simplest means of unifying the diverse elements of Edwards' thought.

Third Question: How Images Arise in the Mind

If vivid preaching is ordained by God as the most suitable means of affecting sinners, how is this kind of preaching related to mental images which may arise in the mind of the hearer, and how does God use these images? Edwards' analysis of various kinds of thought suggests one possible approach to this third crucial question. All speech consists of expressions of a speaker's mind in audible words. The message is initially present in a hearers' mind as verbal sign-thoughts. At this point several things may happen:

1. The hearer may continue to utilize the verbal signs he has received to think about the content of the message.

2. These verbal signs may be translated (by natural means) into sensory signs related in some way to concepts presented in the words. That is, the hearer may envision some aspect of the speaker's message.

3. Either verbal or sensory signs may be translated (by natural means, possibly assisted by the Holy Spirit) into ideal apprehensions. Such apprehensions may be either speculative or affectionate.

4. The Holy Spirit may transpose the ideal apprehensions in the mind of the hearer into a higher order of experience. In other words, He may utilize these apprehensions to produce gracious affections.

Perhaps a concrete example will help. Suppose a preacher is vividly describing the terrors of hell and the imminent danger of souls without Christ. His words are heard and translated into a vivid mental image of impending torment. The force of that vision produces speculative ideal apprehensions that heaven is far more pleasant than hell, and that the salvation offered by Christ is a desirable commodity. It also produces affectionate ideal apprehensions in the form of a lively dread of going there and a desire to have salvation. So far, only natural processes need be at work, although the Holy Spirit may also have been active. Finally, however, the Spirit may transpose these ideal apprehensions into genuine faith in Jesus Christ.

The preaching techniques often employed by Edwards are far more likely to carry an audience through the natural phases of conviction than is an address which is merely cold and intellectual. Vivid, especially sensory preaching, has great potential for producing powerful images in the minds of the hearers. And, if Edwards is correct, it is far more likely to be used by God in the conversion of sinners, because it closely parallels the kind of impact which God's grace makes on the soul. Sensory preaching is not without its dangers, however. The responsibility of a hearer toward potentially idolatrous images has already been discussed. But the preacher is also responsible before God for the images which he attempts to draw for his congregation. It is obvious that he must keep within the limits of truth and propriety, but where are those borders located?

Fourth Question: What Kind of Images to Use

What kind of images should a preacher attempt to paint? It is a difficult problem and one which is not easily resolved, but the preceding discussions do suggest some guidelines. Jonathan Edwards is particularly remembered for images of damnation. However, his theory of primary and secondary beauty and his concept of conversion as a new sight of the beauty of Christ suggest that images of blessedness are also important. As a matter of fact, he specifically notes that preaching is appointed "... particularly, to promote those two affections in them, which are spoken of in the text [II Peter 1:12-13], love and joy..." (Edwards 1959, 116). In some respects, this is the harder task. The natural man can understand judgment, and the preacher may readily find images of terror without consulting the deep things of the Spirit. But who can draw the soul into eternal beauty? Finding the proper images and framing the words and manner to impress them on the souls of men is a spiritual work of the highest order. In that endeavor, two cautions seem particularly needed.

First, there is the danger of encouraging an audience to indulge in mental idolatry. Although a preacher is not responsible for every image conjured up in the minds of his hearers, he ought to be careful not to create verbal portraits of any person of the Trinity. A careful description of God sitting on His throne of judgment appears to be an open invitation to idolatrous imagery. Again, a vivid portrayal of Christ's countenance—for example, as He hung in suffering on the cross, or as He gazed in tender sympathy at the prostitute of Luke seven—this, too, opens the door to a breach of the second commandment.

The second caution has to do with an ever-present danger which stalks any ministry seeking to be affectionate. It is a danger which particularly haunts the preacher who attempts to master the use of vivid images in his messages. That is enthusiasm. Unfortunately, many twentieth century authors have mistaken the affections in Edwards' works for pure emotions. "Affection" is a venerable English word of Latin origin and once possessing a wealth of associations. Only recently has it come to be used almost exclusively for "fondness" or "love." During the Puritan era, it is the common word for "emotion"—a relative upstart on the etymological scene, used in the sixteenth through eighteenth centuries for various kinds of disturbances, including political and physical as well as mental (O.E.D. 1971, 1:853). However, "affection" frequently means much more than "emotion" in the modern sense. Whereas "emotion" commonly refers to an excited mental state and is often identified with the feelings or the passions, "affection" can refer to a more settled state of mind, an abiding disposition or inclination (O.E.D. 1971, 1:39). The religious affections which Edwards seeks to raise involve the emotions, but they are much more; they include a renewed disposition and understanding as well.

It is this which Charles Chauncy refused to believe. In December, 1741, he delivered a Thursday Lecture entitled *The Gifts of the Spirit to Ministers Considered in Their Diversity*, in which he distinguishes four different ministerial gifts. These are preaching to the understanding, to the passions, to the conscience, and (best of all) to comfort distressed sinners. His mood is conciliatory, and he admits that it is proper to address the passions for they are "... capable of serving many valuable purposes in religion, and may to good advantage be exercised and warmed: always provided, that they are kept under the restraints of reason..." (Chauncy 1742b, 8). Within a few short months, however, Chauncy becomes convinced that the restraints of reason have been entirely overthrown. Thereafter, he remains persuaded that the typical subject of the revival is

> ... one whose Mind hath been *greatly terrified* by a *boisterous* Preacher or Exhorter, who hath addressed *only* his Passions, not his *Understanding*; been heaping Terror upon him, without giving him *any clear* and *distinct Account* of the Way to Salvation (Chauncy 1743, 27).

It must be admitted that Chauncy's accusations are not always wide of the mark. Though Edwards disputes his conclusion that the whole work is vitiated by uncontrolled emotionalism, he cannot deny that some problems exist. Edwards' experience with Chauncy suggests that the use of images in preaching must never be divorced from sound reason and solid exposition of the Scripture. In the sermons of Edwards, they are not, but the same cannot be said of all his contemporaries.

Frequently, the charges of mental idolatry and of enthusiasm are properly leveled at the same sermon. Perhaps such productions are most commonly associated with the suffering and death of the Savior. Chauncy cites the example of a Capuchin in Italy who preached "... with a great Rope or Cord about his Neck, and a Crucifix in his Arms..." (Chauncy [1743] 1975, 325), but some Protestant messages are scarcely less vivid or emotional. Detailed descriptions of Roman flogging and crucifixion may evoke powerful images which are followed by waves of pity, but few stop to think that pity is not faith. In fact, pity for Christ is a misplaced sentiment that does not even point toward faith (Luke 23:27-28). This study suggests that preachers be careful to choose images which point beyond themselves. Without such a potential, an appeal to the senses may only produce carnal results.

CONCLUSION

The seventeen forties were a time of religious turmoil. Evangelical renewal struggled with incipient liberalism on the one hand and with suspicious orthodoxy on the other. By the end of the revival, irreversible changes had been effected in the way men thought about their relationship to God. Issues which many had considered settled began to resurface: What is the normal progress of conversion? Is it by seizure, or is a more gradual change to be expected? what is the place of laymen in relation to the clergy? May they preach, and if so, under what conditions? To what extent may individual experience be exalted over the invisible work of God through His covenants? All of these questions have been ably discussed by historians.

One of the neglected issues of the period is the debate regarding mental images of the Lord. Concern over idolatry has surfaced repeatedly throughout the history of God's people. Aaron's golden calf, the iconoclastic controversy of the eighth century, and the Puritan destruction of stained glass windows in Great Britain all give evidence of the passion with which external images of the invisible God have been resisted. However, it does not appear that mental images of the Lord ever became the source of a major controversy until the Evangelical Awakening in Scotland and New England. Although Jonathan Edwards clearly recognized that visions of Christ were not evidence of genuine conversion, he suggested that they were sometimes natural concomitants of a truly gracious experience. In Scotland, Edwards' interpretation was embraced by James Robe as a leading representative of the revival party in Scotland, and vehemently rejected by Ralph Erskine and the rest of the Secession Church. Much of the Scottish resistance to the revival was based on sectarian rivalry, but in the pamphlet warfare over "imaginary ideas of Christ," as the visions were called, deeper theological and philosophical differences became evident. An examination of those differences and their consequences has occupied the pages of this dissertation.

Results of the Study

The results of the study may be summarized by focusing on the contrasts between Edwards and Erskine in four crucial areas: Psychology and Conversion, Metaphysics, Puritan Evaluation of Mental Idolatry, and Preaching.

Psychology and Conversion

Two major differences in the psychology of Edwards and Erskine may be noted. First, Edwards is more empirical than Erskine. Edwards stresses the senses as the fountain of knowledge, while Erskine insists that innate knowledge is the basis for profiting from sense data. Thus, Edwards is more open to recognizing the validity of what actually exists. He observes that some visions are demonic delusions, but on other occasions they are reported by people who appear to be genuinely converted. He further notes that sometimes such experiences appear to be spiritually profitable. Because of his empirical bent, he is ready to consider the possibility of a positive explanation. He interprets them as mental images naturally induced by strong affections. When the affections are truly gracious, the images are potentially helpful. Erskine, however, is determined to reject all mental images of Christ on a priori grounds. It matters not who experiences them. Even the fleeting images which pass through his mind as he writes on the subject call for severe self-reproach.

The second major difference in the psychology of Edwards and Erskine lies in their understanding of the various faculties of the human personality. Erskine is committed to a strict separation of sense (including the imagination) from reason and faith. A saving sight of spiritual realities requires the creation of a new supernatural faculty of perception. Since mental images are related to the world of sense, they cannot help faith. Rather, they are a hindrance to it. Jonathan Edwards holds to a more unitary view of the faculties. Even the supernatural new sense of the Christian does not require the creation of a new faculty. Rather, he describes regeneration as a change in the disposition or habit of the soul produced by the immediate work of the Holy Spirit. Since it is the same undivided soul which both imagines and believes, it is possible for mental images to have a positive bearing on faith. They cannot produce faith; that is the work of God. However, they lie ready at hand and may suitably be used by the Spirit of God for gracious purposes.

Metaphysics

The differences between Edwards and Erskine are more than psychological. They are also metaphysical. Erskine's division of the faculties parallels his adoption of a philosophy known as occasionalism. The substance of the soul is radically different than the substance of material bodies. Since Erskine along with many other philosophers assumes that unlike substances cannot interact, no direct connection between reason and the world or between reason and faith is possible. Common experience suggests a linkage, but that is merely a result of divine appointment. God uses sense data as occasions for improving the innate knowledge of the soul. Thus, Erskine's metaphysics and his psychology reinforce each other in a common rejection of the usefulness of mental imagery.

Edwards' metaphysical system, on the other hand, is a form of idealism which rejects the category of created substance. God is the only true substance. The existence of created beings (both material and spiritual) is dependent not on the continuity of their substances, but on the direct power of God. Since the soul and body are not composed of unlike substances, their interaction poses no difficulty for Edwards' system. Mental images based on a recombination of prior sense impressions can be used by God for spiritual ends without violating the basic nature of either experience. In addition, Edwards' idealism provides him with a world view which suggests an immediate relationship between the physical world and the spiritual world. That relationship is an extension of the biblical concept of the type. His analysis of beauty suggests that the beauty of a mental image of Christ may (at times) function as a type of the eternal and primary beauty of God.

Mental Idolatry

The third contrast between Edwards and Erskine consists of different responses to the problem of mental idolatry. Actually, this aspect of the controversy is more clearly addressed by Robe than by Edwards. The study has suggested that Robe and Edwards hold a weaker view of the dangers of mental idolatry than many of their Puritan ancestors. Considering the wide variety of images which they defend as valid psychological experiences, it is difficult to know precisely which kinds of mental images they might have condemned. Erskine's steady rejection of all imaginary ideas of Christ seems far more in keeping with Puritan exposition of the second commandment. Reflection on the scriptural insights of Edwards, Erskine, the Puritans and Calvin prompts the formulation of guidelines which seem applicable to both external and mental images. The study suggests that portraits of any person of the Godhead ought to be rejected, while historical pictures of the life of Christ may have some limited validity.

Preaching

Finally, the study has drawn attention to a difference in the preaching styles of Erskine and Edwards. This constitutes the fourth contrast between the two. Both men are strongly evangelistic, and both seek to use affectionate preaching to move the souls of men. Besides this, Edwards frequently utilizes vivid, sensory images in his preaching. This technique is justified by his empiricism and by his concept of the parallels between nature and grace. Furthermore, it is noted that Edwards' analysis of thought provides a helpful tool for describing how vivid sermons may be used by the Holy Spirit to produce truly gracious affections.

Relevance of the Study

The principles discussed in this study are relevant to a number of issues facing the church in the twenty-first century. In each case, there is much room for further research.

There are still evangelists and a host of ordinary people who report seeing visions of Christ. Edwards offers a psychological explanation of these events which still leaves room for the gracious work of the Holy Spirit. He challenges the common "all or nothing" approach which insists that visions must be directly from God or from Satan. Edwards, Erskine and Robe all assume that a genuine physical sight of the Lord Jesus is not possible until the second coming. However, they do not provide the detailed scriptural exegesis needed to delineate the characteristics of a genuine vision of Christ, or to prove that no such experience is possible in this age. Even as sober a commentator as F. F. Bruce considers the conversion of Sundar Singh to be a parallel to that of the Apostle Paul (Bruce 1955, 196-97). Yet serious theological questions can be raised about the numerous visions Sundar Singh reported. This suggests that further research into the biblical criteria of actual visions is warranted.

Another important area for investigation is indicated by a rising consciousness of the arts as a valid Christian vocation.

The problems associated with Christian themes in art can be approached from the viewpoint of the artist or from the perspective of the Christian public. If Puritan exegesis of the second commandment is essentially correct, then certain restrictions are placed on the creativity and freedom of the artist. Even if art based on Gospel history is permitted, the artist needs to steer a careful course between two dangers. If he attempts to reproduce a biblical scene as it appeared to a first-century observer, he may miss the inner significance of the event. On the other hand, if he clearly depicts the inner meaning of an event, he runs the risk of obscuring its true historicity (Rookmaaker 1971, 16; La Shell 1976, 70-72). The perspective of the Christian public poses, if anything, an even more difficult problem. In the first place, many Christians are extremely resistant to parting with beloved pictures. Second, many of them find it difficult to make fine distinctions such as those which have been discussed. They want to know if pictures are good or bad—period. When faced with those alternatives, it may be wisest to reject even Gospel history as a proper subject for art.

Perhaps three incidents from the experience of the author will help in illustrating the difficulties frequently encountered among Christians who have never considered the implications of the second commandment. In the first, a chalk artist produced a larger-than-life head of Christ. While his family sang "Beautiful Savior," the room was darkened and the picture fluoresced under ultraviolet light. Then the audience was invited to contemplate the crucified and risen Savior. The atmosphere was charged with emotion; scarcely a dry eye was to be found in the auditorium. The service was followed by eager competition among the young people for possession of the picture, and no one seemed to consider that devotion stirred up by an image might be displeasing to God.

The second incident occurred during a pastoral visit in a home. A grandmother asked her small granddaughter whose picture hung on the wall. The child responded, "That's God." The author realized that an image of God can only teach lies, and that the child had been cruelly deceived. However, it would have made matters worse to tell her that the picture was not really God, but only Jesus, for Jesus is God.

The final incident followed a (perhaps foolhardy) message on idolatry delivered beneath a large stained glass image of the Good Shepherd. One indignant parishioner provided perfect confirmation of the danger of exalting images over the Word of God. Her icy glare was accompanied by the claim that she frequently received more spiritual blessings by meditating on that window than she did from the sermons.

As these examples illustrate, Puritan concern regarding images of Christ has relevance even today. Moreover, if the danger of external images is totally unrecognized in many segments of the modern church, what can be said about mental idolatry? As difficult as it may be, it appears that the subject ought to be addressed. The perils of covetousness and of mental adultery are regularly proclaimed from the pulpit. Perhaps it is time to include instruction on the ways in which men defile God's glory by their vain imaginings of Him.

The final counsel suggested by this study applies again to preachers. If Edwards is correct in admitting mental imagery as a valid aspect of religious thought, those who speak to men for God may properly appeal to vivid imagery in the pursuit of their holy calling. Certainly, any technique can be abused. The preceding discussion suggests ways in which that may happen, but the potential for good is also tremendous. All too often orthodox preachers who are careful expositors of the Word have failed to reach the deeper recesses of the human affections. Modern enthusiasts, with little but zeal to their credit, have produced heat without light. In such an hour, the example of Edwards still speaks. Sermons based on careful exegesis, stiffened by rigorous logic and fired with passionate images may still be honored by God.

BIBLIOGRAPHY

Associate Presbytery. 1742. *Act of the Associate Presbytery anent a Publick Fast.* n.p.

Bizer, Ernst. 1965. "Reformed Orthodoxy and Cartesianism." Translated by Chalmers Mac Cormick. *Journal for Theology and Church* 2: 20-82. New York: Harper and Row Publishers.

Blanshard, Brand. 1948. *The Nature of Thought.* 2 vols. Library of Philosophy. London: George Allen and Unwin.

Boston, Thomas. [1853] 1980. *The Complete Works of the Late Rev. Thomas Boston, Ettrick.* Edited by Samuel M'Millan. Vol. 2. London: William Tegg and Company"; reprint ed., Wheaton, Illinois: Richard Owen Roberts.

Bruce, F. F. 1955. *Commentary on the Book of the Acts: The English Text with Introduction, Exposition and Notes.* The New International Commentary on the New Testament. Grand Rapids: Wm. B. Eerdmans Publishing Company.

Calvin, John. 1960. *Institutes of the Christian Religion.* Edited by John T. McNeill. Translated by Ford Lewis Battles. Library of Christian Classics, vols. 20-21. Philadelphia: The Westminster Press.

Chauncy, Charles. 1741. *The New Creature Described, and Consider'd As the Sure Characteristic of a Man's Being in Christ....* Boston: G. Rogers.

_____. 1742a. *Enthusiasm Described and Caution'd Against. A sermon Preach'd at the Old Brick Meeting-House in Boston, the Lord's Day after the Commencement, 1742, with a Letter to the Reverend Mr. James Davenport*. Boston: J. Draper.

_____. 1742b. *The Gifts of the Spirit to Ministers Considered in Their Diversity; with the wise Ends of Their Various Distribution.... A Sermon Preach'd at the Boston Thursday-Lecture, Decemb. 17, 1741*. Boston: Rogers and Fowle for S. Eliot.

[_____]. 1742c. *The Wonderful Narrative; or, a Faithful Account of the French Prophets, Their Agitations, Extasies, and Inspirations. To which Are Added, Several Other Remarkable Instances of Persons under the Influence of the Like Spirit, in Various Parts of the World, Particularly in New England*. Boston: Rogers and Fowle.

_____. 1743. *The Late Religious Commotions in New England. An Answer to the Reverend Mr. Jonathan Edwards's Sermon, Entitled, The Distinguishing Marks of a Work of the Spirit of God.... By a Lover of the Truth*. Boston: Green, Bushell and Allen.

_____. [1743] 1975. *Seasonable Thoughts on the State of Religion in New England*. Boston: Rogers and Fowle; reprint ed., Hicksville, N. Y.: Regina Press.

_____. 1765. *Twelve Sermons on the Following Seasonable and Important Subjects. Justification... the Nature of Faith... Human Endeavours... The Method of the Spirit....* Boston: D. and J. Kneeland.

_____. 1784. *The Benevolence of the Deity: Fairly and Impartially Considered: in Three Parts.* Boston: Powers and Willis.

Cherry, Conrad. [1966] 1974. *The Theology of Jonathan Edwards: A Reappraisal.* Anchor Books; reprint ed., Gloucester, Mass.: Peter Smith.

Copleston, Frederick. 1964. A History of Philosophy. Vol. *1, Hobbes to Hume.* The Bellarmine Series, No. 16. Westminster Maryland: The Newman Press.

Davies, Horton. 1948. *The Worship of the English Puritans.* London: Dacre Press.

Delattre, Roland Andre. 1968. *Beauty and Sensibility in the Thought of Jonathan Edwards; An Essay in Aesthetics and Theological Ethics.* New Haven: Yale University Press.

Durham, James. 1802. *The Law Unsealed; or, a Practical Exposition of the Ten Commandments. With a Resolution of Several Momentous Questions and Cases of Conscience.* Edinburgh: D. Schaw.

Edwards, Jonathan. [1834] 1974. *The Works of Jonathan Edwards.* With a memoir by Sereno E. Dwight. 2 vols. Revised and corrected by Edward Hickman. Reprint ed., Edinburgh: The Banner of Truth Trust.

_____. 1865. *Selections from the Unpublished Writings of Jonathan Edwards, of America.* Edited by Alexander B. Grosart. Edinburgh: Privately Printed.

_____. 1948. *Images and Shadows of Divine Things.* Edited by Perry Miller. New Haven: Yale University Press.

_____. [1955] 1972. *The Philosophy of Jonathan Edwards.* Edited by Harvey G. Townsend. University of Oregon; reprint ed., Westport, Connecticut: Greenwood Press.

_____. 1959. *A Treatise Concerning Religious Affections.* Edited by John E. Smith. Vol. 2 of The Works of Jonathan Edwards. New Haven: Yale University Press.

_____. 1970. *Original Sin.* Edited by Clyde A. Holbrook, Vol. 3 of The Works of Jonathan Edwards. New Haven: Yale University Press.

_____. 1972. *The Great Awakening.* Edited by C. C. Goen. Vol. 4 of The Works of Jonathan Edwards. New Haven: Yale University Press.

_____. 1980. *Scientific and Philosophical Writings.* Edited by Wallace E. Anderson. Vol. 6 of The Works of Jonathan Edwards. New Haven: Yale University Press.

Elwood, Douglas J. 1960. *The Philosophical Theology of Jonathan Edwards.* New York: Columbia University Press.

Erskine, Ralph. 1743. *Fraud and Falshood Discovered: Or, Remarks upon Mr. Webster's Postscript to the Second Edition of His Letter.... with an Appendix, Especially Relating to Imaginary Ideas of Spiritual Things, Occasioned by Mr. Robe in His Second Letter to Mr. Fisher....* Edinburgh: The Printing-house in the Parliament-close.

_____. 1745. *Faith No Fancy: Or, a Treatise of Mental Images, Discovering the Vain Philosophy and Vile Divinity of a Late Pamphlet, Intitled, Mr. Robe's Fourth Letter to Mr. Fisher*.... Edinburgh: W. and T. Ruddimans.

_____. 1865. *The Sermons and Other Practical Works of the Late Reverend Ralph Erskine, A. M.* 6 vols. London: William Tegg.

Evans, Charles. [1904] 1941. *American Bibliography: A Chronological Dictionary of All Books, Pamphlets and Periodical Publications Printed in the united states of America*.... Vol. 2: 1730-1750. Reprint ed., New York: Peter Smith.

Fawcett, Arthur. 1971. *The Cambuslang Revival: The Scottish Evangelical Revival of the Eighteenth Century.* London: The Banner of Truth Trust.

Fiering, Norman. 1981a. *Moral Philosophy at Seventeenth-Century Harvard: A discipline in Transition.* Chapel Hill: University of North Carolina Press.

_____. 1981b. *Jonathan Edwards's Moral Thought and Its British Context*. Chapel Hill: University of North Carolina Press.

Fisher, James. 1743. *A Review of the Preface to a Narrative of the Extraordinary Work at Kilsyth, and Other Congregations in the Neighborhood*.... 2nd ed. Glasgow: Printed for John Newlands.

Flower, Elizabeth and Murphey, Murray G. 1977. *A History of Philosophy in America*. 2 vols. New York: Capricorn Books and G. P. Putnam's Sons.

Fraser, Donald. 1834. *The Life and Diary of the Reverend Ralph Erskine, A. M. of Dunfermline, One of the Founders of the Secession Church*. Edinburgh: William Oliphant & Son.

_____. Gaustad, Edwin Scott. 1957. *The Great Awakening in New England*. New York: Harper Brothers.

Gentleman. 1742. *A Short Account of the Remarkable Conversions at Cambuslang. In a Letter from a Gentleman in the West-Country to His Friend at Edinburgh*. Glasgow: Printed for Robert Smith.

Gerstner, John H. 1980. "Jonathan Edwards and God. *Tenth, an Evangelical Quarterly* 10 (January).

Gerstner, John H. and Gerstner, Jonathan Neil. 1979."Edwardsian Preparation for Salvation." *Westminster Theological Journal* 42 (Fall): 5-71.

Gib, Adam. 1742. *A Warning against Countenancing the Ministrations of Mr. George Whitefield, Published in the New Church at Bristow....* Edinburgh: Printed for David Duncan.

Gibbs, Norman Brantley. 1953. "The Problem of Revelation and Reason in the Thought of Charles Chauncy." Ph.D. dissertation, Duke University.

Gillies, John. [1845] 1981. *Historical Collections Relating to Remarkable Periods of the Success of the Gospel*, with a preface and continuation by Horatius Bonar. Kelso: John Rutherford, Market Place; reprint ed., Edinburgh: The Banner of Truth Trust.

Goen, C. 1740-1800: C. 1962. *Revivalism and Separatism in New England, 1740-1800: Strict Congregationalists and Separate Baptists in the Great Awakening.* New Haven, Yale University Press.

Griffin, Edward M. 1980. *Old Brick: Charles Chauncy of Boston, 1705-1787.* Minneapolis: University of Minnesota Press.

Haroutunian, Joseph. 1932. *Piety Versus Moralism: The Passing of The New England Theology.* New York: Henry Holt and Company.

Hannay, Alastair. 1971. *Mental Images: A Defense.* Muirhead Library of Philosophy. New York: Humanities Press.

Hambrick-Stowe, Charles E. 1982. *The Practice of Piety: Puritan Devotional Disciplines in Seventeenth-Century New England.* Chapel Hill: University of North Carolina Press.

Johnson, Paul David. 1981-82. "Jonathan Edwards's 'Sweet Conjunction.'" *Early American Literature* 16: 271-81.

Jones, Barney Lee. 1958. "Charles Chauncy and the Great Awakening in New England." Ph.D. dissertation, Duke University.

Kelly, J. N. D. 1978. *Early Christian Doctrines.* Fifth edition. San Francisco: Harper and Row.

Knox, R[onald] A. 1950. *Enthusiasm: A Chapter in the History of Religion*. Oxford: Clarendon Press.

Lachman, David. 1979. "The Marrow Controversy 1718-1723; and Historical and Theological Analysis." Ph.D. dissertation, St. Andrews University.

La Shell, John K. 1976. "Images of the Lord: A Travesty of Deity." M.A. thesis, Talbot Theological Seminary.

Laurence, David. 1980. "Jonathan Edwards, John Locke, and the Canon of Experience." *Early American Literature* 15: 107-123.

Locke, John. 1975. *An Essay concerning Human Understanding*. Edited by Peter H. Nidditch. Oxford: The Clarendon Press.

Logan, Samuel T. 1980. "The Hermeneutics of Jonathan Edwards." *Westminster Theological Journal* 43 (Fall): 79-96.

M'Culloch, William, ed. 1741-42. *The Glasgow Weekly History &c.* Glasgow: n.p.

MacEwen, A. R. 1900. *The Erskines*. Famous Scots Series. Edinburgh and London: Oliphant Anderson & Ferrier.

MacFarlan, D. n.d. *The Revivals of the Eighteenth Century, Particularly at Cambuslang....* Edinburgh: John Johnstone.

McGahagan, Thomas Arthur. 1976. "Cartesianism in the Netherlands, 1639-1676; The New Science and the Calvinist

Counter-Reformation." Ph.D. dissertation, University of Pennsylvania.

Miller, Perry. 1953. *The New England Mind: From Colony to Province.* Cambridge: Harvard University Press.

_____. 1961. *The New England Mind: The Seventeenth Century.* Boston: Beacon Press.

_____. 1973. *Jonathan Edwards.* New York: William Sloane Associates, 1949; reprint ed., Westport, Connecticut: Greenwood Press.

O.E.D. 1971. *The Compact Edition of the Oxford English Dictionary.* 2 vols. New York: Oxford University Press.

Opie, John, ed. *Jonathan Edwards and the Enlightenment.* Problems in American Civilization Series. Lexington, Mass.: D. C. Heath and Company.

Owen, John. [1850-53] 1965-67. *The Works of John Owen.* Vols. 3 and 4: *A Discourse concerning the Holy Spirit.* Johnstone and Hunter; reprint ed., Edinburgh: The Banner of Truth Trust.

Pettit, Norman. 1966. *The Heart Prepared: Grace and Conversion in Puritan Spiritual Life.* New Haven: Yale University Press.

Perkins, William. 1612-13. *The Workes of that Famovs and Worthy Minister of Christ in the Vniversitie of Cambridge, M. W. Perkins.* 3 vols. London: Iohn Legatt and Cantrell Legge, printers to the Vniversity of Cambridge.

Prince, Thomas, Jr., ed. 1743-45. *The Christian History, Containing Accounts of the Revival and Propagation of Religion in Great Britain & America....* Nos. 1-104. Boston: Printed by S. Kneeland and T. Green.

Robe, James. 1790. *Narratives of the Extraordinary Work of the Spirit of God, at Cambuslang, Kilsyth, &c. Begun 1742.* Glasgow: David Niven.

_____. 1743. *Mr. Robe's Fourth Letter to Mr. Fisher, Wherein His Preface to a_ 2d Edit, of His Review Is Considered.... As Also, the Fraud and Falshood of the Reverend Mr. Ralph Erskine's Appendix to his Fraud and Falshood, &c. is laid open.* Edinburgh: R. Fleming and Company.

_____, ed. 1743-46. *The Christian Monthly History.* Edinburgh: n.p.

Rookmaaker, H. R. 1971. *Modern Art and the Death of a Culture.* London: Inter-Varsity Press.

Sang Hyun Lee. 1976. "Mental Activity and the Perception of Beauty in Jonathan Edwards." *Harvard Theological Review* 69: 369-396.

Shaffer, Jerome. 1967. *The Encyclopedia of Philosophy.* S.v. "Mind-Body Problem."

Signs. 1742. *The Signs of the Times Consider'd: Or, the High Probability, That the Present Appearances in New-England, and the West of Scotland, Are a Prelude of the*

Glorious Things Promised to the Church in the Latter Ages.
Edinburgh: T. Lumisden and J. Robertson.

Simonson, Harold. 1975. "Jonathan Edwards and the
Imagination." *Andover Newton Quarterly* 16 (No. 2,
November): 109-119.

Tracy, Joseph. 1969. *The Great Awakening: A History of
the Revival of Religion in the Time of Edwards and Whitefield.*
Boston: Charles Tappan, 1845; reprint ed., New York: Arno
Press and the New York Times.

Vincent, Thomas, n.d. *An Explanation of the Assembly's
Shorter Catechism.* Philadelphia: Presbyterian Board of
Publication.

Wainwright, William J. "Jonathan Edwards and the
Language of God." *The Journal of the American Academy of
Religion* 48 (no. 4, December): 519-30.

Watson, Richard. 1966. *The Downfall of Cartesianism,
1673-1712: A Study of Epistemological Issues in Late 17th
Century Cartesiansim.* International Archives of the History of
Ideas II. The Hague: Martinus Nijhoff.

Watson, Thomas. 1806. *A Body of Divinity, Consisting of
Above One Hundred and Seventy Six-Sermons on the Shorter
Catechism..., with a Supplement of Some Sermons on Several
Texts....* Berwick: W. Gracie.

Webster, Alexander. 1742a. *Divine Influence the True
Spring of the Extraordinary Work at Cambuslang and Other*

Places in the West of Scotland.... Edinburgh: T. Lumisden and
J. Robertson.

_____. 1742b. *Divine Influence the True Spring of
the Extraordinary Work at Cambuslang and Other Places in
the West of Scotland.... Second Edition, with a Preface and
Several Additions in Answer to the Reverend Mr. Fisher's
Review, &c.* Edinburgh: T. Lumisden and J. Robertson.

Willison, John. 1743. *A Letter from Mr. John Willison
Minister at Dundee, to Mr. James Fisher Minister at Glasgow.
Containing Serious Expostulations with Him concerning His
Unfair=dealing in his Review of Mr. Robe's Preface....*
Edinburgh: T. Lumisden and J. Robertson.

Winslow, Ola Elizabeth. 1979. *Jonathan Edwards, 1703-
1758, a Biography.* The Macmillan Company, 1940; reprint ed.,
New York: Octagon Books.

Wyrtzen, Don. 1978. "Jesus is Beyond Imagination." Grand
Rapids: Zondervan Corporation, Singspiration.

Made in the USA
Columbia, SC
08 July 2017